Walks in North Snowdonia

Don Hinson

GWASG Carreg Gwalch

First edition: March 1989
Revised edition: 1997
© *Don Hinson*

Maps are based on the Ordnance Survey Outdoor Leisure Maps
for Snowdonia National Park with the permission of the
Controller of her Majesty's Stationery Office,
Crown copyright reserved.
Every effort has been made to ensure accuracy in text and maps
but the author and publisher cannot accept responsibility
for any inaccuracies.
No part of this publication may be reproduced or transmitted
in any form without prior permission in writing from the publisher.

ISBN: 0-86381-122-1
Printed and published in Wales by
GWASG CARREG GWALCH
12 Iard yr Orsaf, Llanrwst, Wales LL26 0EH.
☎ *01492 642031*

ABOUT THE AUTHOR

Don Hinson was a physics teacher whose chief relaxation was, and still is, walking in the country with his wife. He drew the maps and sketches for this book and she did the typing. He has also written books on physics, *Chiltern Hill Walks, Discovering Walks in Lakeland Mountains, Walks in the Snowdonia Mountains* and *New Walks in Snowdonia*.

CONTENTS

LIST OF WALKS

Note: the last figure in brackets is the total height climbed (1ft — 0.3048 m).

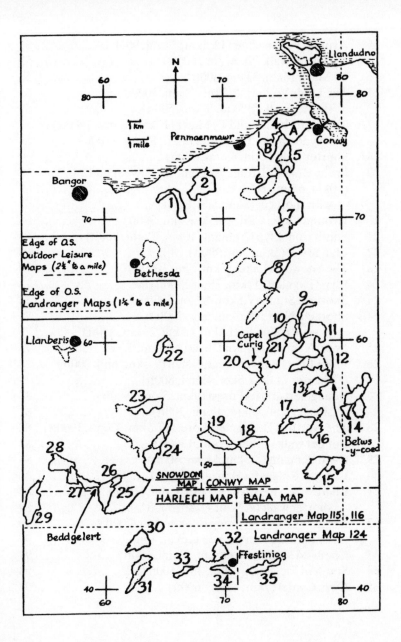

N

80 — 60
80 —
↑1 km
↓1 mile

Penmaenmawr

3

Llandudno

4 A
B 5
Conwy

6

Bangor

1 2

7

70 —

70 —

Edge of O.S.
Outdoor Leisure
Maps (2½" to a mile)

Bethesda

Edge of O.S.
Landranger Maps (1¼" to a mile)

8

Llanberis 60

22

9

Capel
Curig

10 11

21

20

12

23

13

24

17

16

14
Betws
-y-coed

28

26

19

18

15

27

25

SNOWDON
MAP

CONWY MAP

29

HARLECH MAP

BALA MAP

Beddgelert

30

Landranger Map 115, 116

32

Landranger Map 124

33

Ffestiniog

40 — 60

31

34
70

35

40 — 80

Aber Falls

INTRODUCTION

This book describes 35 circular walks, together with many variations. Their lengths vary from 3.5 km (2¼ mi) to 16 km (10 mi). These include 30 different walks in the popular range 5-8 km (3 to 5 mi) while those who enjoy walks over 9.5 km (6 mi) will find 20 to choose from. There are walks to suit all kinds of walkers from those who prefer clear paths in popular scenic areas to the adventurous ones who like to sample more remote regions from time to time. Mountain walks are not included, as they appear in my companion book 'Walks in the Snowdonia Mountains'. Even so, a few walks in this volume are somewhat mountainous in character and provide possible alternatives when the higher peaks are covered by clouds.

Some of its special points are:

●   Routes are chosen to reveal the natural beauty of the landscape with the minimum of difficult, tedious or unpleasant sections.

●   The written route description is always beside the relevant map — not on another page.

●   Route numbers on both map and written description make it easy to relate one to the other.

●   The maps are accurately drawn and easily related to Ordnance Survey maps.

Snowdonia is a splendid and wild area of North Wales, noted for its rugged mountains, remote upland lakes and pools, from which tumble rocky streams and waterfalls, and its natural woods and plantations clothe the lower slopes and valleys. For more details pay a visit to your library — this book concentrates on the walking to keep its price down.

The area covered consists of the Snowdonia National Park north of the national grid line 400, which is just south of Maentwrog.

Walks 1 and 2 make a fine start in the famous **Aber Falls** region, with the bonus of views of the sea and Anglesey.

Walk 3 is not in the Park, but this limestone headland — **the Great Orme** — is much too good to miss.

Walks 4 to 8 explore the **Conwy valley** and show a variety of scenery including that of the coast (the well known **Conwy**

Mountain and **Sychnant Pass**); small mountains (**Tal-y-fan**, with much of archaeological interest); naturally wooded and open valley sides; remote moors and lakes backed by the high mountains of the Carneddau range.

Walks 9 and 10 visit the outstanding beauty of two lakes — **Llyn Crafnant and Llyn Geirionydd**. Many would rate walk 10 as the best in North Wales.

Walks 11 to 13 are in **Gwydir Forest**, which has so many open areas that careful choice of paths gives you frequent views. It is an area of lovely small lakes, old mines and natural woodland as well as plantations and the wonderful **Swallow Falls**.

Walks 14 and 15 explore the pleasant open hills around **Capel Garmon** and the partly afforested remote **Machno valley** respectively.

Walks 16 to 19 explore the lovely **Lledr Valley**, parts of which tend to be neglected in walking books. There are good paths both beside the river and high on the valley sides, and more remote tracks, one of which reaches a rarely visited lake. Historic buildings are also visited.

Walks 20 and 21 are nearer the mountains and take you through a fine variety of scenery (especially no.20).

Walks 22 and 23 are right in the mountains and give superb scenery without too much effort, though paths are often rough. Both walks are graced by lakes, falls and streams.

Walks 24 to 26 reveal the beauties of **Nantgwynant** — a valley along one edge of the Snowdon area with two delightful lakes. It is popular near Beddgelert but walks around Llyn Gwynant are little known.

Walks 27 and 28 in the Beddgelert forest area exploit open or felled areas to give a fair proportion of good views.

Walk 29 explores a pleasant open valley backed by mountains.

Walks 30 and 31 visit little known gently hilly regions west and south-west of the Moelwyn mountains, which can often be seen, together with the shapely peak of Cnicht.

Walks 32 to 35 introduce you to the beautiful, yet neglected, **Vale of Ffestiniog** with its natural woods flanking the valley sides, its rocky streams and tumbling waterfalls.

Llanberis is not in the National Park, but you will find several waymarked walks in the woods of Llyn Padarn Country park and a good 5 mile circuit of the lake, also waymarked.

How to follow a route. A map to a scale of at least 1 inch to the mile and a compass should be taken on walks. Before using this book get to know the words used in the walks descriptions. (See glossary below). Note that 'up' and 'down' refer to gradients (unlike everyday speech when we go down a level road). Read the walk summary when choosing a walk to see if it is likely to suit your tastes and the weather.

GLOSSARY:

Arete: narrow rocky ridge.

Cairn: heap of stones 0.5 m or more in height to mark paths, their junctions and viewpoints.

Col: the saddle shaped top of a pass.

Cwm: upper end of a valley enclosed by steep ground on three sides.

Drive: track to house or farm.

Farmgate: one wide enough for vehicles.

Lane: small surfaced road.

Leat: artificial watercourse that contours round the side of a hill.

On: keep walking in about the same direction.

Outcrop: mass of rock jutting from the ground.

Path: a way too small for vehicles.

Scramble: a steep rocky section where hands are needed as well as feet.

Scree: lots of small rocks a few inches across.

Stile: any device for crossing wall, fence or hedge.

Track: a way wide enough for vehicles.

ABBREVIATIONS

E, N, S, W: east, north, south, west.

Km, mi: Kilometre, mile.

L: left. 'Turn L' means turn about 90°; 'half L' 45°; 'one third L' 30°; 'two-thirds L' 60°; 'sharp L' 135°. 'Fork L' means take the left hand of 2 paths at a junction.

m: metre (roughly a yard).

P: parking off road. Free unless otherwise stated.

R: right.

●: marks a place where there is a choice of routes.

HAZARDS AND PROBLEMS

1. Boggy patches. Wet areas have been avoided where possible, but some patches may be met. I can't promise that the ones mentioned in a walk will be the only ones you find — conditions vary from year to year.
2. The more mountainous walks (6, 8, 22, 23) should not be attempted in snow, ice or mist.
3. Since many lowland walks have rocky or rough sections wear suitable footwear with thick soles to ensure comfort and safety.

MAPS

Most walks are on the 1¼ inch to the mile Ordnance Survey Landranger Map 115 (Snowdon). Walk 14 and a small part of 15 are on map 116 (Denbigh and Colwyn Bay). Walks 30 to 35 are on map 124 (Dolgellau).

The 2½ inch to the mile Outdoor Leisure Maps are optional alternatives with the advantage that they mark walls and fences. But be wary of paths marked in green as some of them are simply not there. If the green is printed on top of black dashes, the path is much more likely to exist.

Maps needed for each walk are listed after the title of the walk. Letters refer to Outdoor Leisure Maps: B – Bala; C – Conwy Valley; H – Harlech; S – Snowdon.

Note that the maps in this book show details useful for following the route described, but unnecessary details (e.g. stiles and walls met on an obviously clear path) may not be drawn in.

Main route ━━━	Building ■	Bridge ≈
Alternatives ·-·-·-·	Wood ◌	Stream ⌇
Road ═	Fence ⌐⌐⌐	Lake ⬭
Steep ground	posts only ''''''	Marsh + +
Summit ▲	Wall ━	Railway ⋯
	broken ····	
Cairn ▲	Stile ×	km grid lines
Crag or outcrop ʺ	Gate ⌐	65
Boulders or scree ⋰		57

Map symbols

11

Grid references are given for the starting points of the walks. The first 3 numbers refer to the grid lines showing how far East the point is; the last 3 numbers to how far North. Thus on walk 1, 663 means the start is three tenths of the way from the vertical line 66 to line 67, and 720 means the start is on line 72.

Buses run by the start of many of the walks, at least in the summer. Check the timetable before attempting to use them. Note particularly the summer Sherpa buses which give access to many walks.

Trains stop at Conwy, Dolgarrog, Betws-y-coed, Pont-y-pant, Dolwyddelan and Roman Bridge.

How the routes were chosen. This book is the result of a fairly comprehensive survey of paths during a continuous period of over six years. I have tried to link the scenic, fairly dry and comfortable paths into circular walks of various lengths to suit all tastes. Apart from the fully described and mapped walks, including over 400 km (250 mi) of routes, comments on the existence and state of a further 100 km, (62 mi) of paths are made. I hope this will make it easier for those who wish to explore new routes to decide what paths are worth trying.

I am grateful for information from Gwynedd County Council, Snowdonia National Park Office and the Forestry Commission, which has helped me sort out a few footpath queries, and especially to my wife for typing the manuscript and to Mr D. Salter for useful comments on the routes.

CHECKLIST OF ITEMS TO TAKE ON WALKS

Rucksack with food, drink, first aid; walking boots, socks; clothes adequate for wet, cold or windy weather; map, compass; watch; money; keys. Optional: camera, binoculars, pencil, notebook.

Check the weather forecast (e.g. phone Llanberis (01286) 870120).

For excursions into more remote areas make sure food is ample in case of delay and take whistle (in case of accident).

Llyn Idwal and Twll Du, The Devils Kitchen

1 ABER

(9.5 km, 6 mi, 800 ft) Map 115, S.

Summary. After a gentle climb up a delightful valley to the impressive Aber Falls, Rhaeadr-fawr, you pass the smaller Rhaeadr-bach. Soon the return becomes a most attractive high level track along the valley top. The longer walk bears L and carries on at a high level parallel to the coast with good views across to Anglesey. Paths are mainly good though there will be some small wet patches after rain. There is a short rough scramble near the falls.

The high level path going N towards Aber is not correctly shown on the map but my route keeps as near to it as possible. Also near Plas-nant (645 717) the path is overgrown so a minor detour is needed. (I have not used the attractive path at 644 709 as there is a marshy patch and a barbed fence to cross).

Parking. From Aber drive SE along the lane to the car park near the bridge (663 720). There is limited parking in Aber. Buses run along the coast road. Abergwyngregyn is the full name of the village.

1 At road bridge take the footpath by the river (on your L) until you cross a footbridge. **2** Here bear R up the valley track. **3** Just before reaching the falls, cross the stream and scramble up the boulders. Make for the stile and carry on (roughly W) along path with fence (and/or wall) on your L. **4** On over stream coming from the smaller falls. Go through gate 100m further on. **5** Before path gets close to wall go half R along small path. It crosses stream and goes up a small hill. **6** Keep on when path fades. At top of the rise the path is seen again and goes through an old wall gap. (Stream along far side of wall). **7** Here bear R along a track with old wall on the R. **8** Over stile by gate and up, soon with 2 fences on your R. **9** Through gate and on along a clearer track under pylons. **10** After passing animal shelters you reach a track junction. ● Here turn half L to pass through gap in pine wood. Soon on over stile. **11** Follow track as it bears R just before a gate. (Ignore the track that goes on reaching the pylons after 250 m). **12** After crossing stream track turns L to gate. Here leave track and go down field with stream on your L until you

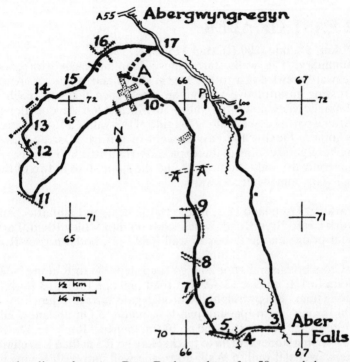

reach a line of stones. Bear R along these for 50m and then go
half L down path soon with fence on your L. **13** When fence turns
L you go half L towards barn. Just before barn bear R along a line
of trees and down to house. Pass just R of house and go along
track over field. **14** Keep on track as it bears R (up) then L. **15**
Fork L down track to pass just L of houses. Then go over field
and along by a hedge (on your L) soon passing through a small
gate. **16** Stay on path when fence goes down away from it. Soon
ignore stile on your L unless making for the coast road. **17** Turn R
along lane.

1A A Shorter Version. (6.5 km, 4 mi, 700 ft)
Follow the main walk to stage 10, but at the track junction go
down track until it is just about to enter the pines near the bottom
of the wood. **A** Here turn sharp R along path towards the R side
of Aber. **17** Turn R along lane (or L to reach coast road).

2 EAST OF ABER

(9 km, 5¾ mi, 1200 ft) Map 115, S, C.

Summary. The walk starts above Llanfairfechan with good seaward views down to the Menai straits and Anglesey. After crossing an attractive valley you climb open fields to reach a dramatic view down the valley in which Afon Anafon flows. After a partial descent along the side of this valley a Roman road is joined. Finally, the easy descent of a ridge (Garreg Fawr) makes a good ending to this exploration of a little known area. A generally dry walk. Some may find the stone steps in two of the tall walls somewhat awkward.

Parking. Go inland (SE) at the traffic lights in Llanfairfechan. Fork L into Bryn Road, which leads on into Valley Road. Park near bridge and letterbox in wall (689 742), both on your R.

1 Cross bridge and after 20m go L up steps. Turn R along lane. Soon fork L up lane. **2** At next road junction turn L. **3** Fork L along track. Keep straight on through gate at track T-junction. **4** On through farm, passing just L of house. **5** On up lane 70m. Here go half R over stile and on 100 m, then half R to gate. Down to stepping stones and up to track. Here go R 3 m then L to climb steps over tall wall. **6** Walk up beside wall until wall begins to bear R. Then keep on over field between 2 rushy areas, and bear L to stile which is 150 m L of house. **7** On over this stile walking by wall on your R. **8** Over stile in fence and down slight path near wall on your R. This wall bends slightly R 50 m after passing 2 trees. Here bear L keeping fairly level over grass to find a small but clear path within 50 m. It goes towards L edge of distant plantation. **9** 50 m before the first pylon fork one third R down slight path. Then make for stone wall 20 m R of where it is joined by slate wall. Down awkward steps and L up lane. **10** At lane end go L beside wall (on your L) soon joining a track that turns R near pylon. **11** At top of long gentle rise turn L along track past 2 pylons. The track goes to the R side of a small ridge. **12** At a wall corner fork R along a gently falling track. **13** After track bears L ignore a sharp R turn. Follow wall on R until it turns R. Here follow grass track that bears away from wall but returns to it at

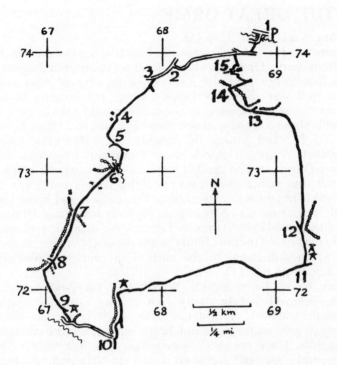

small gate. **14** Sharp R through gate down path. 50 m before a small gap go sharp L down path to farm. Make for stile L of farm. **15** Over stile, then turn R between fence and hedge. Go L down drive to road. Turn R back the way you came.

Other paths near this walk. The path going SE from 695 740 to Bwlch y Ddeufaen at first climbs near an attractive stream. It then becomes vague at times, with some wet patches, as it climbs the featureless moor.

3 THE GREAT ORME

(8 km, 5 mi, 900 ft) Map 115

Summary. This splendid limestone headland lies just outside the national park. 'Orme' may have meant sea monster or dragon. It is a real Wonderland, not just because the original Alice lived here and was visited by Lewis Carroll, but because of the numerous areas of geological, archaelogical and natural interest. Fossils abound in the quarries. Stone age man lived here before 12,000 BC and among BC remains are a Neolithic burial chamber (4 upright stones and a capstone), long huts, and Pen-y-Dinas, an iron age hill fort with some ramparts and hut circles, but rather overgrown. Neolithic copper mines can be visited. They were later worked by the Romans and in the 18th and 19th centuries. A spring at Ffynnon Rhufeinig (Roman Well) was used to wash the ore. Tudno, a Welsh missionary, built a church around the 6th century on the site of a present one, parts of which date back to the early 13th century. (Summary continued on p.20)

More recent items include Wyddfyd (a very old cottage), Pen-y-mynydd Isaf (a partly 17th century farm), a unique funicular tramway, cabin lift and ski slope (1987). A good variety of plants grow on the grassland, heathland, limestone pavements and cliffs. There are also two public gardens. Sea birds can be seen, and sometimes grey seals. Goats are often sighted. (They have become so numerous that some have been moved elsewhere e.g. near Llyn Gwynant). Booklets giving more detail can be bought at information centres.

This walk passes near to most of these features and there are splendid high level views of the cliffs, sea, coast, Anglesey, mountains and town. Paths are dry and in most places very clear.

Park at the West Shore as near the start of the Marine Drive as you can (769 822). (Or a short distance along Abbey Road (772 822) where a footpath leads up to a level path. Turn R and follow instruction 2 onwards.)

1 Walk along the coast road with the sea on your L and turn sharp R up path after passing Gogarth Abbey Hotel. ● **2** Enter Haulfre Gardens and at once go L up steps. At fork go up L. At next fork go R along top edge of gardens. **3** Turn L up steps 50 m before

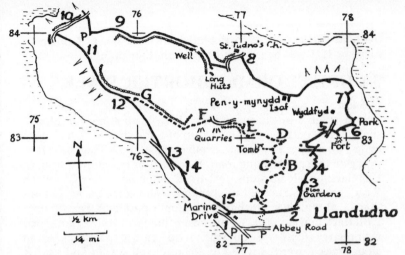

end of gardens. On through gate along fairly level path passing just R of golf course. (Ignore minor side turnings.) **4** Down winding steps and R along road. Cross tramlines and turn L beside them. Very soon join path on R that runs parallel to the tramlines. Just before building, follow the U-turn, to join path along cliff base. **5** At road go up it 50 m and turn R along path for 20 m. Then turn L with path (or go on to explore hill fort) and 50m later fork L down. **6** Through small gate into park. At once turn L along path for 50m, then again L up steps. **7** At top of rise turn R away from path for sea views, then turn L to the top of the small hill. Now aim for the clear path well R of Orme summit. (To R of this path is steep ground). Follow this path as it bears L, but just before house go R through gate and along track. **8** Near the church turn L up road then R over grass to join track beside wall. **9** After bearing gently L and R the wall turns L. At this corner carry on over grass bearing slightly L to reach surfaced track. Go R down it to road and L along it. (At road you can cross over to view cliffs and birds). **10** Pass a gated wall gap. At the next (ungated) wall gap go L up a small path. It becomes vague as you pass just R of car park. **11** Soon follow gently rising green path with steep ground not far to your R. Soon there is a wall on your L. **12** At a small grassy bank across the path turn one third R down grass path that soon runs down the hillside to the road. **13** 100m down the road turn half L along a track. **14** At fork (without gates) take R fork gently down. **15** Turn R down to road, or L if you began the walk at another point.

3A GREAT ORME: SHORTER WALK

(4.5 km, 2¾ mi, 700 ft)
Follow stage 1 of the main walk. Turn L up steps just after a shelter. The path zig-zags up a strip of gorse shrubs. When steps end go on over grassy area to climb more steps. **A** Then bear R to iron gate and go on along road. **B** Soon after bus stop turn sharp L up lane and R up steps. **C** Turn R along lane. (At Cromlech Road, go along it to see burial chamber and come back). **D** Turn sharp L along track which bears L then R past café. **E** Soon bear L off track and along grass path beside fence on your L. Join road near quarry (fossils). Soon, when road bears R to hotel, keep on along track towards sea. **F** Go down to wall corner and bear R beside wall. **G** When small post is seen 100 m ahead bear L over grass to reach, and turn L along, clear path running down hillside to road. Then follow 13 to 15.

4 CONWY MOUNTAIN, MYNYDD Y DREF

(15 km, 9½ mi, 1300 ft) Map 115, C
Summary. This mountain is reached by a long gentle climb from Conwy with splendid views of both sea and mountains. It is crowned with an Iron age hill fort that has ramparts up to 5 m thick and many hut circles. After reaching the top of the Sychnant Pass you can, if you wish, make a fine high level circuit of the valley of the Afon Gyrach and Foel-lus. The return passes a small reedy pool before a more rural return through fields. Other optional extras include visits to Allt-Wen or the Druid's circle, a Bronze age ring of stones 25 m in diameter. The walk is particularly attractive when the extensive areas of heather are in bloom. A mainly dry area usually with few wet patches.

Parking. Go W out of Conwy on the A547 coast road. Soon (150 m) after leaving the town walls turn L over railway and R along road that soon bends L. Watch for Mountain Road and turn R along it. There is a small parking area at its end (774 778). The

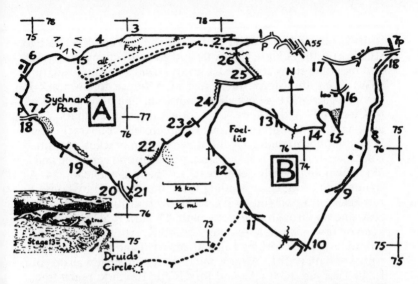

town can also be reached by bus or train. Both halves of the walk can be tackled from the top of the Sychnant Pass where there is parking (749 770).

1 At the end of Mountain Road fork one third R up footpath. **2** Turn sharp R along small crossing path or, if not found, R along clear path. On reaching the crest of the ridge turn L up it. Follow paths on or near crest. Pass just R of the sloping rock face. **3** The final steeper rise is on a small path just R of crest. After this rise regain the crest to go through the hillfort. **4** Go down a winding track towards a distant farm. **5** Take the R fork along a path passing near the top of a deep valley on the R. Just past this top keep on (ignoring a L fork). Soon the farm is seen again. **6** At wall bear L to walk beside it with the wall on your R. Later turn L along track. (When near the pass a detour up a rough path will soon reach Allt-Wen.) ● **7** Cross the road and take the wide path (SW) that keeps R of the wall and near power lines. It follows a fairly level course across the hillside. **8** Watch for a fork. Take the L fork gently up (not R down) to a track at top of wall. Follow track SW near poles. **9** Ignore path going gently down by wall. Instead fork L along level path. Later ignore a smaller path going off L and stay on a wide (at first vague) path that crosses a wet patch well supplied with stones. **10** At wall turn R by it. When it turns L, you go half L down path to bridge and up (NW) path to stile over wall. **11** Here cross stile and go half L along grass track and on along stony track. (Detour to Druid's circle: go sharp L (SW) along this stony track; just after house follow track R through gate and L near wall on your L; at sign post take R fork to Circle.) **12** Track goes gently down through 2 pillars. **13** A grass track comes up from your L and crosses your track. Here keep on for 50 m then go half L down path in bracken past small tree. (See drawing) Over tiny stream at a dip and gently up and L along winding nearly level path to the ridge ahead. **14** At signpost go down clear winding track that bears R by house to run beside a wood (on its L). **15** Sharp L at junction. **16** Over road and on through gate along path. **17** Turn R along road, but keep on up track when road turns sharp R. After passing houses ignore level track forking L. **18** Cross road and go through gate with wood on your L. After wood, follow path near wall on your L. **19** Pass just R of lake and fork R for 100 m to reach track. Keep on, and at once fork L soon going down track. **20** On along road 100 m then turn L through gate just before house. (If there is a wet patch, railings can be used to get across.) **21** Pass through small gates you see ahead, and later one slightly to your L. Then go half R towards wide gate with a wood beyond it. **22** Pass just L

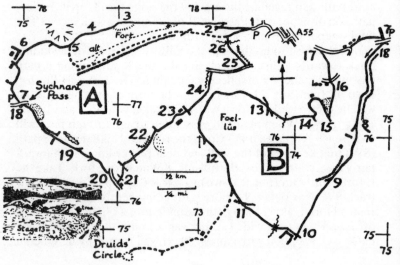

of wood. Turn R along lane which soon turns L. **23** After passing large buildings on your R, then on your L, turn R along lane for 30 m and L at footpath sign. **24** 100 m before houses go half L to road and R along it. **25** Go sharp L at footpath sign (fence on your R). Go on to gate and bridge as fence bears R. **26** Go up to track and R along it.

SHORT VERSIONS

(both about 7.5 km, 4¾ mi, 650 ft).
(A) Conwy Mountain only. Follow 1 to 6, then 18 to 26. For a quick return bear L after descending from the fort to pick up a rough track with a wall on its R. (Total 4 km, 2½ mi.) Or for better views use a clear path parallel to this track but higher up.
(B) SW of Sychnant Pass. Park at top of pass and follow 7 to 17.

5 SOUTH FROM THE SYCHNANT PASS

(10 km, 6¼ mi, 900 ft) Map 115, C
Summary. This high level walk is largely in open country with extensive views of the beautiful Conwy Valley. At its southern end you pass the old Llangelynnin church (see walk 6) and later walk through woodland which is largely deciduous on your right with occasional glimpses of the valley through the trees. (On the left is a dense plantation). The paths are usually dry and easy to follow. One section is a little difficult with a minor detour to avoid crossing barbed wire; it has an alternative which is easy but misses good views. (See stage 9) At point 5 a short cut down the lane to point 18 saves you 2.5 km (1½ mi).
Park E of the top of the Sychnant Pass where the two walls that enclose the road end (754 769).

Other paths near this walk. The track ESE from the old church goes roughly down in the wood to 758 733 where a path goes NE near the lower edge of the wood. The E-W path through 760 741 in the wood has gone.

1 Facing Conwy turn R along the main track past lake. **2** At T-junction turn R. Ignore sharp L turn to house, but soon fork R at track junction. **3** When main track bears away from wall on your L fork L along track by wall. **4** Stay on track when wall bears L. The wall is back by track later on. Later the wall again bears L and comes back. **5** Bear L with wall to iron steps R of gate. ● Over steps and along path with wall on your L. **6** Ignore stile for house on L. Keep on over grass through wall gap and past house on R. Soon there is a wall by your R. **7** On over stile at stream. Go across field to gate and stile. Here go on by wall on your L. **8** On along track that soon bears L through gate. Just after gate turn R over field to stile. Go along enclosed path, then down drive to lane and over stile. **9** For the easy alternative route go half R up to stile and then L to pass church and soon go along track between walls; follow stage 15. Otherwise go L up vague paths in bracken to farm gate in fence about 80 m from lane. **10** Here go gently down field to climb stone steps in wall by some boulders. **11** Bear R up field to go through farm gate and follow fence (on your L) until it descends to a fence junction. **12** Here go half R (E), at first parallel to old wall. (No path). Go gently down until slope steepens and track is seen. Here turn R down easier slope to reach another track. **13** Go L down track and R along track that soon passes just R of house. **14** When wall on your L turns R go through gate and half L over field to gap in old wall. Follow small path, soon by forest edge. Pass just R of house. Soon track is reached. **15** Go down track 50 m into wood and then L along clear path which winds (mostly down) through wood. **16** Go half L down path past farm. Over stile and L along drive, then on up road. **17** Ignore rough track on L and later turn R at T-junction. **18** After 30 m turn L through gate and up field near fence on your L. Through gate and L up drive which soon bears R. **19** Fork R to pass R of house. **20** At barn bear L up rougher track passing L of barn. **21** At junction (before house) turn R up track. **22** At gate fork L up grass track to house. Then bear R to pass R of house. **23** Fork R to return the way you came.

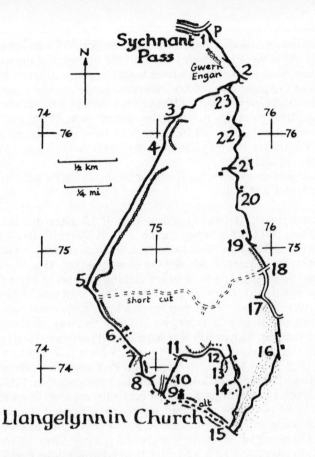

6 TAL-Y-FAN

(10 km, 6¼ mi, 1800 ft). Map 115, C.

Summary. This walk abounds in ancient remains. These include the impressive Maen-y-bardd burial chamber and various standing stones. The alternatives 2 and 3 also reach a small stone circle, and Barclodiad-y-Gawres, an oval heap of stones which is another ancient burial chamber. Alternative 1 passes the two circular ramparts of Caer bach hillfort. All routes pass the remote old Llangelynnin Church, founded in the 7th century, with the spring of water in the corner of the churchyard once used

25

for baptismal purposes, and its 16th century porch. There are still occasional services held here. Much of the first part of the walk (to point A) is on the Roman road from Chester to Caernarfon. Views of the great Carneddau mountain range are seen and of the beautiful Conwy valley. Although the sides of Tal-y-fan have few features, its rocky ridge to the summit is most enjoyable. Anglesey and the sea can be seen from here too. Routes are usually fairly dry, but may have wet patches between 4 and 5, and between 10 and B.

Park at Rowen in layby on L beside footbridge (just before Ty Gwyn Hotel 759 719).

1 Go up road. At road junction fork R. **2** Keep on up at T-junction. Watch for burial chamber on R 700m (½ mi) after Rhiw (Hostel) and standing stone on L 100 m further on. (There is another stone later on R). ● **3** On along road for 60 m, R over stile and on up slight path. You are making for a small dip in the skyline beside a distant wall junction. **4** Over wall stile. After a large rushy area on your R you reach a fork. Either way can be used but the R fork is drier. Posts show the way over some wettish patches. **5** Over stile just beyond wall junction. Turn L by wall and soon half R along path to stile. **6** Over stile and turn R along path about 10 m from ridge wall. Pick your way carefully up through boulders and later down a short steep section. **7** After summit you can follow path when it gently moves away from wall (on your R) or stay by wall until a detour L is needed at a steep drop. **8** When wall turns one third R, go over easy grass to a rocky knoll 150 m ahead. (Detour R if ground is wet). Close to knoll bear L to pass just L of it and bear R to go down grass beside a line of boulders and small outcrops on your R (NE towards Conwy Castle). **9** Soon a ruin is reached where you bear R along small path towards a wall. ● **10** On by wall (on your L). When wall bends L leave it and keep on (E) down to col. (No path. Easy grass if you dodge the gorse. Take care not to fall into a small mine entrance). **11** Near col go L along clear track that soon gently descends, later passing through two gates beside enclosures. **12** Ignore rough track going down L and keep on to stile. (Visit Church now.) Here bear R off track and walk on grass (wall on your L) 50 m to gate and stile. **13** On over grass

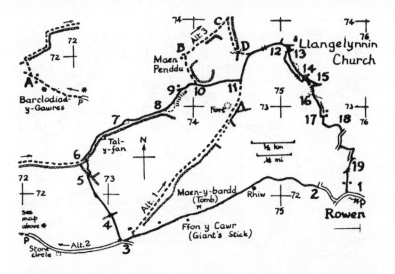

roughly parallel to wall on R. You may need to detour L round marshy area. **14** Ignore stile on R but cross stile 50 m ahead. Go down path with old wall on your R. **15** 50 m after house go sharp R for 50 m until near house. Then half L down field with line of boulders kept on your R to stile between streams. **16** Over stile and down track, soon by fence on your L. **17** Just after house go L to more houses and R along lane that soon turns L. **18** R along road for 150 m, then L through gate and along field edge. Through small gate at corner and R (with hedge on your R). **19** On along drive 100 m then L over stone step. Over field to buildings and gate. On along lane and L down road.

Alternative 1.

(9 km, 5½ mi, 1200 ft)

To avoid climbing the mountain follow 1 and 2. Then turn R through gate marked Cae Coch (100 m before road) towards house. Soon turn R along rising path with wall on your R. When wall at last turns R, keep on by old fallen wall, soon joining good wall. At triangular enclosure bear L with track to col. The track soon gently descends, later passing through two gates beside enclosures. Now follow 12 onwards.

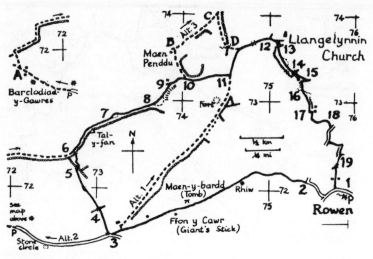

Alternative 2.

(12.5 km, 7¾ mi, 1900 ft)

To extend the walk to Bwlch y Ddeufaen follow 1 and 2 and go on
along road. At stone steps in L wall a small stone circle can be
visited. Barclodiad-y-Gawres is 400 m beyond end of surfaced
road. Beyond this are the standing stones (one on each side of
the track) after which the pass is named. (Ddeufaen – two
stones.) **A** Here go half R over grass to wall and cross it at a dip.
Follow this ridge wall (on your R) later on a path, past the stile at
a shallow col. Keep on up boulders and down short steep section.
Then follow 7 onwards.

Alternative 3.

(an extra 1 km, ½ mi).

To visit Maen-Penddu, follow 1 to 9 then turn sharp L at wall.
Follow wall down (on your R) until it bears away R. Then keep
on (roughly N) to the massive 2 m high stone Maen-Penddu. **B**
There turn R along track. **C** 200 m after wall near your R bears
away R, turn sharp R along path beside wall (on your L). **D** At
wall gap and stream, go through gap, over stream and along
grassy track soon joining the main track. On through two gates
beside enclosures. Now follow 12 onwards.

Looking towards the Carneddau Mountains

7 AROUND LLANBEDR-Y-CENNIN

(11 km, 7 mi, 1300 ft) Map 115, C.

Summary. The walk can be started from Rowen following the pleasant Afon Roe for a time, apart from a detour (optional) to climb a small hill for good views of the Conwy Valley. After going through the attractive village of Llanbedr-y-cennin, with its simple medieval church, old tracks take you fairly gently up into the hills for a visit to Pen-y-gaer. This Iron Age fort has 3 ramparts. Below its main entrance in the SW you will find many pointed stones set in the ground. These 'cheveux de frise' slowed enemy charges down so that defenders had more time to launch their missiles (arrows and stones). The return goes gently down the open hillside back to the quiet village of Rowen. There are good views of the valley in the higher sections of the walk; also the Carneddau range of mountains are seen from an unusual angle. Paths are usually mostly dry except at stage 14.

Park at Rowen in layby on L beside footbridge (just before Ty Gwyn Hotel 759 719). For those wishing to reach Pen-y-gaer sooner there is limited parking in Llanbedr-y-cennin a little E of Ye Olde Bull (761 695). They can shorten the walk to 6 km, 3¾ mi, 1100 ft at stage 19 by forking R at lane junction.

1 Cross footbridge and go on, soon between walls. **2** Just before iron steps turn L along by hedge, then R to walk by river (on your L). **3** Unless you wish to stay on the road to point 7, turn L over road and R down steps. Go on over field the way the steps point, to a gate just L of house. **4** On along grass and through concrete farmyard to white farm gate. On over stream to another farm gate. On 15 m then go L up field with wall on R and poles. **5** At field corner cross the low but rather awkward fence and go up field towards house. Then bear R to walk by iron fence. At hedge go L and at once R over stiles. **6** Go one third R to steps in hedge on crest of ridge. Go on down with hedge on your L. At next hedge go through the R hand of 2 gaps and follow hedge (on your L) down to barn. Go on through gate just R of barn to road. **7** Go on across road, over bridge, and past houses to iron steps. Here go L to walk by Afon Roe. **8** Just after bridge on L go over stile. Cross field keeping near farm on R. **9** Over stile near house and L to gate. Keep on with hedge on your R. **10** On along track, then road, past church to Ye Olde Bull. **11** Here fork R up lane and soon fork L. **12** At Bryn y Coed fork R up rough track. Go R through farm gate by pole and L along faint field path. Bear R by hedge (on your R) up to barns. **13** Here go L between barns and R along grass track passing just L of house. **14** At next barns turn L up stony track. (If muddy go through gate on R beside pens and follow faint path in bracken parallel to track). **15** When wall on L ends follow wall on R to leat. Go on by leat. **16** Turn R over first bridge and on along track. **17** Go R up ladder stile over wall. The fort is reached after crossing wall at a second stile. Return to this stile but turn R along wall without crossing it. **18** Soon a wall stile is reached. Here turn two thirds R down the L of two banks. Keep on when bank ends to reach gate into lane. **19** Down lane. ● Fork L at lane junction. **20** As lane bears L, cross stile over wall and go N over field to pass just L of large pylon. Here a grassy track leads to house. Use gate just R of house to reach road. **21** Turn L along road for 100 m, then R between walls. Keep on over field with wall on your R. When wall bears R keep along clear path. When path becomes narrow make for ladder stile over wall about 100 m ahead. **22** Over stile and on, soon beside sunken lane on R. **23** Over iron steps and down by fence and lane

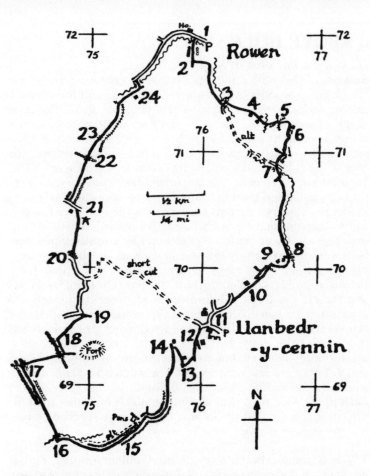

on R. Join track at gate. **24** Pass just L of house. Soon turn L to road and R down it. Ignore turnings off to the L.

Other paths near this walk. The path S from Rowen is good until Gors-wen is reached. After this paths are very bad. The path NE from 762 715 is hard to follow. The path SW from 765 691 near Tal-y-bont that follows Afon Dulyn has little value. It can be muddy; the waterfall can hardly be seen; and paths W from the falls are hard to follow.

8 ABOVE DOLGARROG

(12 km, 7½ mi, 1900 ft) Map 115, C.

Summary. This walk can be split into two contrasting parts, one on the steep wooded slopes above Dolgarrog and the other in remote uplands with reservoirs not far from the Carneddau range of mountains. The stiff climb up in attractive natural woods is relieved somewhat by a zig-zag path. Then a Roman road is followed towards Llyn Cowlyd before climbing over the Moel Eilio ridge into the valley that contains Llyn Eigiau. (This burst through its dam in 1925 and filled Llyn Coedty reservoir. In turn this collapsed sending water down to devastate Dolgarrog killing 16 villagers). An easy track returns you past Llyn Coedty. Then a descent may be made beside Afon Porth-llwyd, with its impressive falls, or (rather less steeply) by a winding old lane. Not everyone will enjoy this strenuous walk in which the huge black pipeline is so often evident. Others will enjoy these industrial wonders, including the leats, tunnels joining reservoirs and the railway track. (Before the roads were built, men and materials were hauled up a steep incline and then travelled on a railway from near Llyn Coedty to Llyn Cowlyd. The railway was used until 1968. Only the sleepers remain now.) The route is mostly easily followed, but note instructions carefully at stages 8 and 9. There are few wet patches. The worst is at 20 and can be avoided by using the alternative descent.

Park in the wide road near the bridge just N of Dolgarrog (769 678) or in a space just up the side lane. Can be reached by bus, but the railway station is a mile away.

1 Walk S from the bridge towards the Aluminium works. Turn R up side road that soon bends L. **2** Carry on over pipe line and turn R just after crossing next bridge. **3** After coming close to pipe for 50 m turn L over stile and up zig-zag path. **4** Cross stile by a tree and turn L then R to next stile. Over this and R under first pipe. Then L up steps. **5** At iron shed turn R along clear level track. ● **6** On along road, then fork half L up track. **7** Keep on at top of rise, with mountains and Llyn Cowlyd in view. **8** When the good track runs into rushes bear R between rushes and bracken to the L end of a wall. Here go up path in bracken (at 45° to fence). Soon a

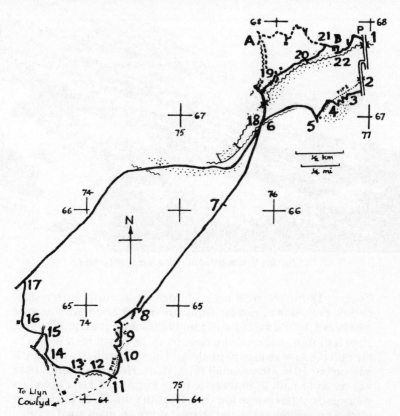

small flattish open grassy area is reached. Here go L down (SSE) to ruin. **9** At R corner of ruin take a small path that goes S down in bracken. It keeps just L of reedy area. Over stream and on to end of wall. **10** Here follow path down to pipe then up to stile. Over stile and L down track and under pipe. Then follow grass track (not the stony one). **11** At track junction go R to stile and on up. Follow vague path on R of stream. It bears L to stile. **12** Here keep on up path between rushes (on L) and bracken. **13** Go through wall and bear slightly R (NW) for 60 m then slightly L (W). Soon a col is reached. **14** Down by wall (on your L) until path swings away from it. **15** When path returns to a wall go through gate down path to house. **16** Pass just R of house and follow track down. **17** Turn R at junction. Later pass Llyn

Patches of snow on the hillside above Llyn Cowlyd

Coedty. **18** Follow road across bridge. Soon turn R over stile. Follow path down, not far from stream. **19** Soon after second stile bear L by old wall to wall gap. Follow wide grass path to gate 50 m R of ruin, and on down clear path. **20** Watch for a R turn to the falls if you wish to explore them. Then carry on down to reach an iron bar 10 m after 5 small stone steps. Here bear half R over wet patch to path in bracken leading to stile. **21** Here go down stony path. After house (on your R) path turns R. **22** Go L down track. At junction take the R road down to main road.

SHORT VERSIONS

(A) Uplands and lakes (8.5 km, 5¼ mi, 900 ft). Park just past Pont Newydd (759 670) after a drive up a steep narrow road. Follow 6 to 17. (A circuit of Llyn Cowlyd could be added. See below. A short cut can then be made at a 'walking man' post (737 640) NNW passing L of square fold).

(B) Woods and falls (3.5 km, 2¼ mi, 1000 ft). Follow 1 to 5. Turn R at road and follow 18 to 22.

Alternative descent (adding 1 km, ½ mi). At stage 18 don't use stile. Stay on road a further 100 m then turn R on path by leat (kept on your L). **A** At road turn R and very soon R again down old lane. Turn L with lane when nearing house. **B** Much further on path turns R after passing house (on your R). Then follow 22.

Other paths near this walk. Of the paths between Dolgarrog and Coed Gwydir (780 642) the only other one I could find to climb the steep slopes was the surfaced one just N of Afon Ddu (774 663). The footpath along the valley just N of Afon Ddu tends to be wet. The path W from 736 644 to Llyn Eigiau is hard to follow. Paths E of Llidiard-fadog (762 679) are too poor to enjoy. The path SE from point 20 (763 676) has wet patches. Paths near the bridge over Afon Ddu at 767 658 are often wet and hard to follow. For walks to Llyn Dulyn, Melynllyn and round Llyn Cowlyd see p.97-98.

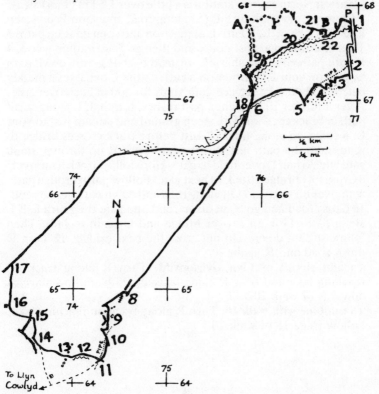

9 LLYN GEIRIONYDD FROM TREFRIW

(6 km, 3¾ mi, 600 ft) Map 115, C.

Summary. After a steep climb through the village a path takes you more gently up the side of the Crafnant valley. Although wooded at first, the trees gradually thin out until your high level route gives splendid valley views. At the lake the walk can be extended by making a circuit of Llyn Geirionydd or following walk 10. After a short rough descent beside a mountain stream and past an old mine building, an easy track takes you down the valley. The final path beside the Afon Crafnant is delightful and reaches impressive waterfalls near the end of the walk. Paths are usually pretty dry.

Park opposite Trefriw Woollen Mill (784 630). Buses stop here. Llanrwst North railway station is a little over 1.5 km (1 mi) away. **1** From the car park turn L (S) along road and soon R up steep lane which bears L. **2** Turn L at junction and soon go R up path. **3** Turn R down road past house and then go L up path in wood. **4** Ignore path going up sharp L. Instead bear R gently down path by wall on your L. Further on a path on the L bypasses a muddy patch. **5** ● At lake retrace your steps for 200 m back over stile. After a further 100 m, when past rushes, turn half L along small path in bracken, soon with steep ground and stream just to your L. **6** Keep on along track. **7** Just before track crosses bridge to road, take the path just R of bridge. Turn R up through small gate and go half L over field to gate. Here follow track near river. **8** Cross tiny bridge 10 m L of next gate. Follow path through gate, with river on your L. **9** On along road and down path near its end. **10** Cross road and go 50 m down road opposite then turn half L along path. **11** Turn L over bridge and L again to falls. Then follow stream down. Do not cross the next bridge. **12** Turn R down road and R again.

To add circuit of Llyn Geirionydd. Turn R along track on reaching lake and bear L along lakeside path. Follow stage A onwards of walk 10B.

To combine with walk 10. Turn R along track on reaching lake. Follow stage 15 of walk 10.

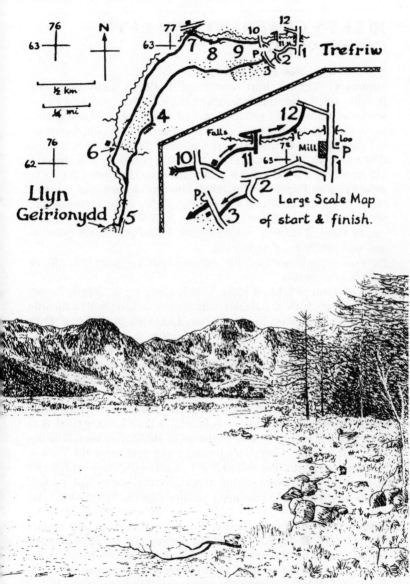

Llyn Crafnant and its attractive background of hills

10 LLYN CRAFNANT AND LLYN GEIRIONYDD

(9.5 km, 6 mi, 600 ft) Map 115, C.

Summary. After a short road climb beside a rocky mountain stream, you reach the beautiful Llyn Crafnant, backed by an attractive hummocky group of mountains. After a lakeside walk a pleasant stream is followed before turning back. A climb on an old path, paved in places, gets you over the wooded ridge and down to Llyn Geirionydd. The full walk climbs gently through old mines to a little known path with splendid views across to mountains and down to the lake. The final return also has fine views down the Crafnant valley. The walk can be shortened or lengthened to suit all tastes. By using walk 9 to reach stage 14, it can be tackled starting from Trefriw. Paths are mainly good — any wet patches are soon over.

Park in car park (not free) just below Llyn Crafnant (756 618), or near N end of lake.

1 Go up road to lake. **2** Here turn R along track. **3** Into forest, soon taking L fork. **4** After passing the end of lake, watch for stile on L. Here go along field past ruin and through wall gap. Path bears L, soon by stream. (If too wet, return to track and carry on to next stile.) **5** Near house, turn L along track. **6** Turn L along road. ● **7** At phone box go half R along path. It soon bears R uphill and into forest. (At top, note the viewpoint just R after wall gap.) **8** After a short descent go down forest track for 50 m, then down wide path off to L of track. This crosses the track twice more. (If wet use track instead of path). **9** Turn L along track that later bears R along the end of the lake. **10** At road turn R along path beside road. Carry on up road when path ends. **11** Turn R steeply down path that soon turns L. Later go L over bridge and R up road. **12** Turn L along track passing house (on L) and reaching old mine. **13** Pass just L of spoil heap and cross stile. The path rises then drops to the lake. (Note the perched block on the skyline.) **14** On along path just R of road. At end of lake turn L along track. ● **15** Just after old monument to Taliesin (6th century poet) on R, turn R up grass over a wet patch and on up grass track. It winds down to wall. **16** Here go over low gate and, 50 m later, fork L up path through a small rock outcrop. **17** Up through wall gap. **18** After mine go down forest track.

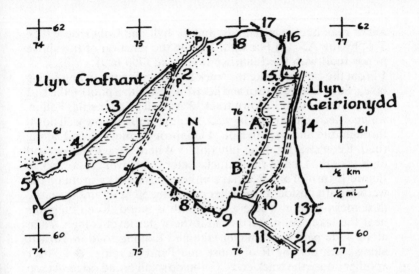

SHORTER WALKS

(A) Round Llyn Crafnant (5 km, 3 mi, 100 ft).
Follow 1 to 6, then stay on road.
(B) Round Llyn Geirionydd (5 km, 3 mi, 200 ft).
Park on the road somewhere near point 10, 12 or 14. Follow stages to 14, then bear L along path by lakeside. **A** Just after mine scree, the path climbs steeply up and soon down again. **B** At field carry on along level path. Turn L at track and follow stage 10.

11 GWYDIR FOREST LAKES AND MINES

(12 km, 7½ mi, 1200 ft) Map 115, C.
Park (1) For walks 11 and 11B by Llyn Sarnau (778 592) on the

minor road between Llanrwst and Ty-hyll, the Ugly House (756 576) by the A5. (2) For walk 11A by the junction of the above minor road with the Llanrhychwyn road (790 609).

1 From the car park take the track L of Llyn Sarnau (when facing lake). Soon ignore L turn and keep on now with a pool on the L. 2 At field on L, turn R down track. 3 At wall go over stile. Follow waymarked path, at first by wall. At next house follow wall down through fold and over to stile. 4 Up through mine. Turn L along road. Keep straight on at junction. 5 Where 2 tracks leave road on R take the L hand rising track. Later go on over cross-track. 6 Ignore L turn. Turn R at lake either on the rocky arete or the wettish path beside it. In either case after 50 m scramble up the next rocky section where a good path is found. Keep on paths near the lakeside, or further in if the water level is high. 7 On along wide path past smaller lake and L along road. 8 Turn R along track passing R of house and Pandora mine. ● 9 After another house the track ends. Go on up small broad ridge. At top bear L to follow old wall kept on your L. 10 Bear R to farm gate in fence and on down grass track in shallow valley. Near wall make for gap R of farm gate and go down between walls and on down field. 11 Through farm gate and along path, then track and lane. 12 When lane bears L keep on over field until 50 m past church just on your R. Here go R through small gate and down field passing 2 houses on your R. 50 m below second house go through small gate. 13 At track turn L past house and soon R through farmgate. Cross field (fence on your L) to go through farmgate. Here follow track bearing R, with wood not far R. 14 At end of pines just on your R, go half R along path keeping wall on your L. It soon turns L. 15 Turn R along lane. 16 Turn R at the next road junction. Soon fork L up surfaced track. 17 Turn R along fairly level unsurfaced track. 18 Turn L along road and soon R at track below Hafna mine. At once go L along base of waste heap. Follow path that bears R along L edge of mine passing steeply just L of buildings. (For an easier route stay on road and later go sharp R up track to top of mine.) Near chimney bear R along path that soon turns L up to top. 19 On up track and on over ladder stile. ● 20 Turn L along fairly level winding track. 21 Later note turning to viewpoint only on L. Then watch for and go one third L along path gently down.

11A AROUND LLANRHYCHWYN

(7.5 km, 4¾ mi, 1100 ft)

Walk up the road and soon fork L up surfaced track. Follow
stages 17 to 19. Then keep on up path. **A** At top near house turn L
20 m along track and R along path. Go down in pines, over track
and down path to Llyn Glangors. **B** Follow the R hand line of
poles to gate and on to second gate near mine buildings. Here
turn R along track, later passing house. Now follow stages 9 to
15.

11B A SHORTER LAKES AND MINES WALK

(7 km, 4½ mi, 400 ft)

Follow stages 1 to 8. Just after mine buildings turn R through
gate and up field near L line of poles. Through gate and on by
poles to Llyn Glangors. **B** Pass just R of lake and up path in
pines, soon crossing track. **A** Near house turn L 20 m along track
and R along path. **20** Turn R along fairly level track and follow
stage 21.

41

Summary. Four of the many small lakes are seen on this walk, which exploits the many open areas in and around the forest. Starting at the beautiful Llyn Sarnau (which sometimes dries out in the summer) an open path takes you past Llanrwst mine (see summary of walk 12) and later through Cyffty mine which has remains of interest. A track through felled forest brings you to the peaceful Llyn Bodgynydd and an interesting lakeside path leading to its smaller companion. After another mine, Llyn Glangors is seen as you climb over a hill and down to Llanrhychwyn with its simple old church with parts dating to the 12th century and the rest completed in the 16th. The font is perhaps the oldest in Britain. The church was used by Llywelyn Fawr, the great ruler of Gwynedd in the 12th century, and his wife Joan. A descent of a quiet lane gives scenic views of the Conwy Valley and the Grey Mare's Tail waterfall. Then a track takes you by a pleasantly reclaimed mining waste area. Next along the forest edge to climb through the Hafna lead mine workings, and finish along a short enclosed section with a viewpoint. A largely dry route, usually with few wet patches.

Other paths near this walk. A pleasant (but soon enclosed) path runs NE from point 9 passing down through a mine to point 13. The path N from 788 600 tends to be overgrown and is losing the good views it once enjoyed.

Llyn Sarnau

12 SWALLOW FALLS AND LLYN PARC

(15 km, 9½ mi, 1100 ft) Map 115, C.

Summary. Although this walk is in the Gwydir Forest, there are plenty of open stretches. A delightful riverside walk soon brings you to the magnificent Swallow Falls. Look back at the falls as your path now runs high above the river. Soon you climb still higher with fine views across the deep valley of the Afon Llugwy. Later a splendid aerial view of Betws-y-coed can be seen from Clogwyn Cyrau — a rocky outcrop with a sheer drop to the east. At Betws-y-coed a track takes you north with views of the Conwy valley before climbing the impressive Aberllyn ravine to reach Llyn Parc. Now a forest path takes you to Llyn Sarnau, near which you can detour to look at the ruins of Llanrwst mine. A board shows plans and details of this lead mine. A pleasant path with good views gets you back to a minor road near the old Cyffty mine, also with ruins of interest. Then all that is left is an easy downhill walk on the little-used road. Normally paths are pretty dry, except by Llyn Parc (see stage 16). **Park** up the minor road that leaves the A5 by Ty-hyll, the Ugly House (15th century). There is parking at the start of the first forest track on the R (757 577) or 1.5 km (1 mi) up the road at the viewpoint (766 584). The walk can also be joined from Betws-y-coed. (Car park near bridge 792 567 is not free.) Trains stop at Betws-y-coed.

Other paths near this walk.

The obvious direct route from point 8 to 9 was uneven and overgrown at 778 578. The path along the wood edge from 776 577 to 778 580 and then W to 773 582 is good. A pleasant path runs W from Coedmawr to the next forest track (782 584).

An open view towards the mountains seen on walks 12A and 12B

1 Walk down the road. **2** Just before road bridge go L down steps. Follow path by river. Soon after ladder stile the path goes on along the field edge. **3** Just after Swallow Falls follow the L of two paths near river. It climbs away from the river but soon returns to run high above it. **4** Turn L up track. **5** Just after house go half R down path. Turn L 100 m after crossing bridge and soon R up steps to road. ● **6** Go up path just L of house. At far corner of garden turn R gently up hill to fence. Turn L to go up by it, now on a faint track. **7** Turn R through gate and along edge of wood, then up into it. **8** Over field and on along winding stony track by barn. Turn L at track T-junction and R at the next two T-junctions. **9** 50 m after a grass track joins yours fork L to gate and on along grass track up field. Stay 10 m from wood edge on R when track fades. Pass between barn and house and follow clear track. ● **10** Turn R at junction and soon L along track, later passing a group of buildings. **11** At T-junction near building, turn R to go through gate and soon L down winding track. **12** When track ends go on to top of slight rise for views from crag top. Return to track but soon turn L up path. Later path descends to old fence (on your L). **13** Here turn L down wide path in dark pines. After passing through wall gap follow path as it zigzags R then L. Go on down track. ● **14** At track junction keep L up hill. **15** Just after top of rise, go half L up path. Keep on over a crossing path. **16** At Llyn Parc go on beside its edge. (If too wet, keep on the track on R of lake, bear L at junction and follow stage 18.) **17** 15 m before iron pipe near end of lake, turn R along path in ferns. Soon fork L gently up path. Keep on along track. **18** Take L fork. After a short descent turn half L down path to track. Bear L along it a short way, but keep on along a path when track turns R. The path is roughly level apart from one short drop and rise. **19** The path rises into dense pines and goes through wall gap. Use path on the L to get round wet patch. Bear R along track and go on over crossing track. (Or turn R to explore Llanrwst Mine.) ● **20** Turn sharp L at junction along track between pools. At field on L, turn R down track. **21** At wall go over stile. Follow waymarked path, at first by wall. At next house follow wall down through fold and over to stile. **22** Turn L along road. Keep straight on at junction.

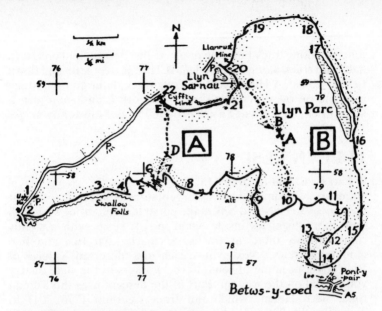

12A SWALLOW FALLS

(10 km 6¼ mi, 800 ft).
Follow stages 1 to 9. **10** Turn L at junction. Keep on over crossing track. **A** At Coedmawr use stile just to its R to cross field up to stile. **B** Turn L along track, soon forking R up. **C** After passing house, turn L at track junction and go down track at first in pines. Now follow stages 21 and 22.

Shorter version. (5.5 km, 3½ mi, 500 ft).
Follow stages 1 to 5. **6** Go up path just L of house. Soon go up into wood. **D** After leaving wood turn L along track and soon half R up field. Follow markers through gateway and past house. **E** Follow wall down to ladder stile by old mine and up to road. Now follow stage 22.

12B LLYN PARC

(9.5 km, 6 mi, 700 ft)
Park in Betws-y-coed. From the A5 cross Pont-y-pair bridge and turn L past car park and soon R up lane. At junction go on up forest track and follow stages 15 to 19. **20** Turn sharp L at

junction along track between pools. **C** Just before field on L turn half L up track along forest edge. **B** Turn R over stile and down field to house. **A** Here keep on along track, later going through gate and on over a crossing track. **10** Fork L and soon turn L along track, later passing a group of buildings. Now follow stages 11 to 13.

13 LLYN ELSI

(8 km, 5 mi, 800 ft) Map 115, C.
Summary. This upland lake is largely surrounded by forests, but open areas to its N and NW make possible a delightful walk with only short distances inside woodland. It starts with a steady climb, mainly on clear tracks, to reach Llyn Elsi and fine mountain views. Next you reach the deserted village of Rhiwddolion, home of some of the workers in the slate quarry you passed on the way up. Part of the descent uses the Roman road, Sarn Helen, which ran from Caerhun (776 704) to Trawsfynydd (706 387). After climbing Miners' Bridge the walk ends along a riverside path by the lovely Afon Llugwy. Paths are mostly good, but there may be short wet patches between points 4 and 5. Also, just before 14, avoidable by joining Sarn Helen near 13.
Park on the wide A5 about 200 m W of the bridge (Pont-y-Pair 792 567) in Betws-y-coed.

1 Walk along the road away (W) from village and turn L up a track. **2** Cross stile by gate and go on up track through old quarry. **3** At building, follow track sharp R. **4** 40 m before farm, turn sharp L along track. Soon cross stile on R and follow path which soon crosses forest track. **5** At monument Llyn Elsi is seen. (For a closer look use the path, often wet, and track along its E side. Then turn back to the monument.) Retrace your steps to the forest track. **6** Here turn L along track. Ignore first turning down on R. **7** Turn R at T-junction. 50 m past next junction turn L through gate to Pant-yr-hyddod. **8** Pass just L of house and on up short steep grass slope. On over grass, keeping just R of reedy area. Aim for stile into forest, but before reaching stile turn R to join track 50 m R of forest corner. **9** Turn L along track down to

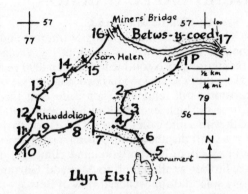

gate and on. **10** 50 m before next gate, turn half R along vague track for 20 m, then go R over hillock to low wall. Cross this and go down to small gate. **11** Here go on along a clear path, then turn L through gate to ruin. **12** Here turn R past converted chapel and through felled forest. **13** Go on across track and down track bearing R past farm. Then go down grass by wall on your L and down a line of flat stones that bear away from the wall. Soon a rough track is joined which zig-zags to run by a stream. **14** Turn R over bridge and soon join and descend the rough track — Sarn Helen. (Or stay on L of stream and turn R at next track then L down Sarn Helen.) **15** Go on over a crossing track. **16** On over the A5 road and up Miners' Bridge then turn R along riverside path. **17** Turn R over bridge and R along road.

Other ascents are inside woodland most of the way. The track going up just R of St Mary's Church leads to a good path that turns R off it at stone post. The final stages are often wet. Another path starts up stone steps near our parking place on the A5. It has one or two spectacular viewpoints, but is harder to follow.

14 AROUND CAPEL GARMON

(15.5 km, 9¾ mi, 1700 ft) Map 116,C.

Summary. This walk has many points of interest and can easily be shortened in several ways. Starting at the village, the first feature is the impressive Neolithic tomb over 4000 years old. The central oval chamber 3.5 m long has two side recesses over one of which a capstone still remains. Then a descent through fields brings you to an old high level track with good mountain views. A pleasant path with a fine valley below it takes you to the A5. This is joined for a short distance before using a path giving access to the lovely Fairy Glen. Next a woodland climb, an open forest track and a further gentle climb to Mynydd Garthmyn. From here there is a splendid almost aerial view of Betws-y-coed, and a fine prospect of mountains. The Conwy Valley stretches out to the N and is seen again as you circuit Moel Trefriw before the final descent. Paths are usually fairly dry, though the track in section 4 can be muddy. Mud near 17 can be avoided.

Park near church in Capel Garmon (816 554). Other places: below Fairy Glen (799 546); layby on A5 (809 536).
1 From the parking area by toilets, turn L (S) along road. ● **2** Keep on at road junction. Later turn R along drive (signposted to burial chamber) to Tyn-y-Coed. **3** Near farm (on your R) bear L through gate with signpost to small gate and on to tomb, which is fenced round. **4** Passing just L of tomb, follow small gates and signs S to reach a track. Follow this (R) down through farm. **5** Here turn R along lane. It bears L and reaches rough open ground. **6** Here turn R along rough track. Later pass R of mast. **7** Turn L along track soon passing house on your R. ● **8** Then go half L through small gate and down path. Later keep near wood on your R. **9** Go down path in open ground. After steep descent, ignore path going down on R. Your path runs parallel to the A5, soon with a wall on its R. **10** Turn L along track at buildings. Soon go up the A5 (no pavement). Turn very sharp R down path. Later a path opposite hut on your R allows a detour into Fairy Glen. **11** 100 m before track bends R, turn R along drive towards Cwmanog Isaf. Use gate on R to pass just R of house. Go through next gate and turn R to follow wall up to road. **12** Cross road and go up path slanting up slope. Watch for the sharp L turn

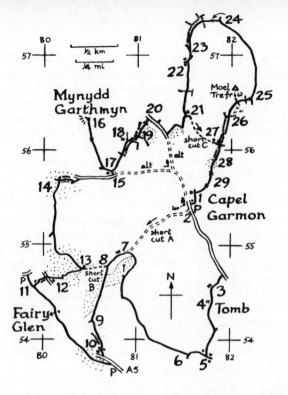

and follow zig-zag path up to track. **13** Here turn L. **14** About 0.5 km (¼ mile) past a track junction, watch for a path crossing your track. Turn R up it between wall and stream. Turn L along drive, then R up lane. **15** Just before phone box, turn L up path by wall, and L along drive through iron gates. After 50 m leave drive and go on up clear grass path in bracken. **16** 100 m before wall and pine wood, fork L to rocky viewpoint. (The actual summit is a short way SE.) Retrace your steps towards the phone box. **17** Just before drive joins lane, turn L along track. (If too muddy, use the road instead. Then turn L at T-junction; R up lane with wood on your R; follow stage 21.) When track ends at gate, keep on near fence on your R. This bears R to a stile and gate. **18** Go over stile and follow wall on your R which turns R to wall gap. Go through gap and at once L, soon into wood. **19** The path bears away from wall at a wall gap. It then runs down to slate slab bridge and iron gate. Go through and up field by hedge on your L. **20** Turn R along road. Pass by drive on L, but turn L up lane with wood on your R. ● **21** When near farm at a sharp R bend leave lane and go half L to pass just L of house. Go on over field and through gate 80 m below top of field. **22** Go through gate just R of buildings and soon R along track through farmyard. Then on along the L and lower of 2 tracks. **23** Soon ignore L fork down to gate, so you keep on with fence on your L. Track bears R so that it aims just R of mast, and ends at gate. Here keep on over field to small gate. **24** Here on to second small gate and R up track. **25** When track reaches its highest point it turns half L at gate on your R. Go through this gate and on over fields crossing 2 low fences and keeping R of rushy area. Bear L to gate. **26** Here go through gate and on near fence on your R. After a slight descent go R through gate and L down to ruin. Over fence and stile, then half L over track to gate. **27** Through gate and half R along field edge, but skirting round a rushy dip. On over field towards pines and small gate. **28** Through gate and go R for 10 m then L along path by poles. Over stile and down field by poles. **29** Over stile and down track by poles. Turn L at cottage to reach gate and keep on to car park.

SHORT CUTS. One or more of these may be taken.

(A) Omitting tomb (saves you 3 km, 1¾ mi, 200 ft). Follow stage 1 only. **2** Turn R at road junction. **7** Keep on at road end along track past house on R. Now follow stage 8 (and on).

(B) Omitting Fairy Glen (saves you 3 km, 1¾ mi, 500 ft). Follow stages 1 to 7. Then carry on down track into wood (ignoring track going off R) and follow stage 14 and on.

(C) Omitting circuit of Moel Trefriw (saves you 2.5 km, 1½ mi, 400 ft). Follow stages 1 to 20. Stay on track until ruin with tree fallen on roof. Here go half R to gate and follow stage 27 and on.

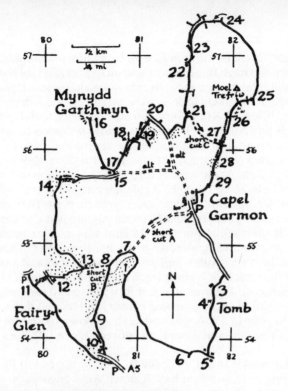

15 AROUND PENMACHNO

(12.5 km, 7¾ mi, 900 ft) Map 115, 116, C.

Summary. The walk starts with a circuit of Moel Pen-y-bryn, the shapely partially wooded hill close to the village. A pleasant path takes you along the valley in which the Afon Glasgwm flows. Then a climb brings you to a scenic high level track above the remote Machno valley. After crossing the river by bridge, a further climb on the other side brings you through forest before the final descent with a fine view of Penmachno and its quiet and beautiful valley. The paths in this walk are generally dry and easy to follow. In the Church are some very early Christian tombstones, one probably A.D. 540, and there are several old farmhouses near the walk.

Park near the Church (790 506).

1 Start along the road signposted Ty Mawr. **2** Go up to the road junction. Here go through gate on L and join path beside poles. **3** Leave poles to go through gate and on to pass just L of barn. Bear R to slate slab bridge and L over it, soon along clear track. **4** Pass through farm, then fork L over bridge. Go down drive over second bridge. **5** After house, go on over fields and into forest. **6** Bear R down track. **7** Turn L just before house on L. At stile go half L up path. Just after iron 'shack' up in a tree, bear L 100 m up path to track. **8** Up track. At junction turn sharp R. **9** Keep on at next junction. At cross roads turn L. **10** At junction fork R down. ● **11** Go R along road. **12** At signpost turn L over footbridge. Follow stream until bridge where you cross it. Then make for stile by gate. There turn half L, soon passing just L of cottage. **13** Bear R up track at junction. **14** Into forest, later turning L at track junction. **15** Ignore the grassy fire break on L, then fork L where the track divides. **16** Turn L at road and soon R along lane. **17** At junction fork L along track that at once turns R. **18** Turn L at T-junction. **19** Cross stile just R of house and turn one third L across field to small gate near corner. **20** Here go down field by wall on your L. Cross stile and keep on down by stream on your L. **21** Cross lane and down path between fences. **22** Turn L along road.

Shorter version (8 km, 5 mi, 600 ft). Follow stages 1 to 10, then go on along road and turn half R down wide grass path.

Other paths near this walk. The path S from Pont Oernant (786 495) is pleasant but turning sharp L at 784 488 takes you E up one that soon deteriorates. Cwm Penmachno is an attractive area, but too many of the paths are missing, and a circular walk cannot be made. A good track runs SW from the bend in the road (753 472) up through old quarries. It is not possible to cross by the old reservoir (748 464) to join the route going E.

Many paths SE of Afon Machno have gone except near Penmachno or where they are drives to houses. Adventurous walkers could go SW from 830 516 to Hwylfa; follow the wall NW to a fold (811 517) and turn SSW past Ffridd-wen after which paths are clearer. The packhorse route from Penmachno to Ysbyty Ifan is there and is surfaced after 823 489. From this point good routes can be followed NE to the road near Ty Mawr (502 837). From here I don't recommend the path NE near Afon Eidda. Then the path NW by Afon Conwy is attractive but ends at a barbed fence near 832 519.

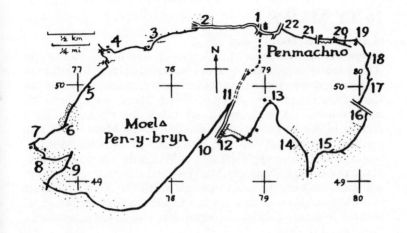

Moel Pen-y-Bryn, the hill beyond Penmachno village

16 TY MAWR

(6 km, 3¾ mi, 800 ft) Map 115, C.

Summary. A splendid start near a lovely and rocky river — the Afon Lledr — is followed by a forest climb that is rewarded at the top by extensive valley views backed by mountains, including the Carneddau range. You also pass Bwlch Maen, a pleasant 17th century house. A high level track takes you through a short section of forest before your descent to Ty Mawr. This late medieval farmhouse was the birthplace of William Morgan, writer of the first complete Bible in Welsh. It was published in 1588. The cottage (National Trust) is open at certain times. Next you walk the hanging valley through which the Afon Wybrnant flows before the final descent to the Lledr valley. Fairly short sections in stages 2 and 4 can be muddy. Use of stones or banks avoid most of this.

Park just E of the railway viaduct that crosses the A470 4 km (2½ mi) S of Betws-y-coed at 781 538. Parking is limited here. An alternative at 775 522 where a track crosses the road, is best reached from Penmachno. (The track is reached after driving past an area of open moorland on the R.)

1 Walk away from viaduct a short distance and turn sharp R over wall down steps and along path. Cross bridge and bear L along path to wall gap. **2** Here turn L along track near river. Later the track climbs and leaves river. **3** Cross road and turn R up path in trees. Later go straight on over track. **4** Follow path sharp L up to house. Go over gate just L of house, bear R round it and along track by stream. **5** At clear track turn sharp R along it. Soon fork R along edge of forest. **6** Go down road, passing Ty Mawr. **7** Soon after a track crosses road, the road turns R. Here keep straight on through gate down rough track. After passing house, the track turns R. Here go back if parked by viaduct. Otherwise turn R along track which later climbs and leaves river; then follow 3 onwards.

Other paths near this walk. The forest tracks from 799 539 running SW to point 6 are too enclosed at first to be enjoyable. Paths and tracks SW of Bwlch Maen seem to have gone. So has the path S until the forest is reached at 785 521. The path between Bwlch Maen and Fedw-deg is clear in the wood but vague and often muddy outside. A good route NE by the river is reached by crossing a fence (not barbed) at 783 535.

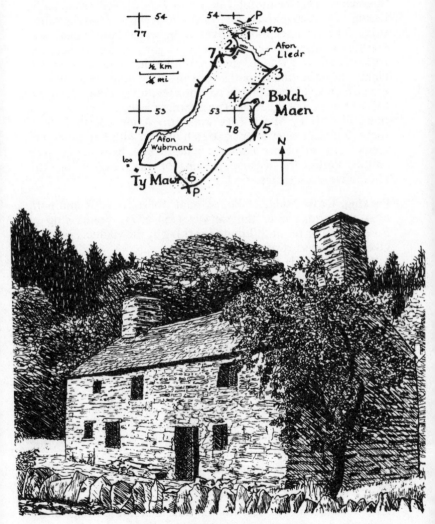

Ty Mawr, birthplace of William Morgan

17 THE LLEDR VALLEY

(12.5 km, 7¾ mi, 1000 ft) Map 115, C.

Summary. This beautiful valley can be enjoyed from paths beside its attractive river and from high level routes on the valley sides. The best section of river is between Pont-y-pant and Gethin's Bridge. There is an impressive gorge and elsewhere the rock-strewn river is a delight to walk beside. After a fairly stiff climb, the little known paths N of the river join up to make a scenic high level route, while part of a forest road does the same for the return S of the river. The alternative walk climbs another fine valley to Ty Mawr. (See walk 16.) After a further climb through pines a remote open stretch of land with fine mountain views is crossed before a descent in more pines back to the Lledr valley. Paths are usually reasonably dry, except on the alternative walk (stages C, D).

Parking. Cross bridge at Pont-y-pant, follow road R and park near the bridge over the railway (754 537). Trains stop at Pont-y-pant on request. Limited parking by the viaduct (781 538) gives another starting point for the walks.

1 Walk E towards the bridge over the river but keep on at the junction instead of going L over bridge. **2** Go on down rough track when drive turns R into Outdoor Centre. Soon cross drive and go along track with wall on your R. (If wet use field on your R.) Path soon runs near river. **3** Through gate. Here you can follow vague and wet paths near the river to enjoy the narrow rocky gorge it runs through. Or go on up in pines to the top of the rise then turn half L along path, which soon returns to the riverside. **4** Near bridge go R 50 m over 2 stiles and L along drive. Just before bridge turn R along track. **5** Over stile and on along small path near poles. **6** At end of field go up grass track. Soon go under railway. **7** Follow fence (R) and wall (L) to house. ● **8** Here turn sharp L along track between walls. When track turns R go half L to cross bridge and follow path to road. **9** Go L up road under railway then R along track. **10** Soon turn L up small path in bushes. Later keep on up track. **11** Fork L off track to cross small bridge. Turn L at track. **12** At track junction take the L fork. Later on again fork L. **13** Turn L at far end of house and go down path. Keep on (vague path) to barn, turn L for 20 m, then R to

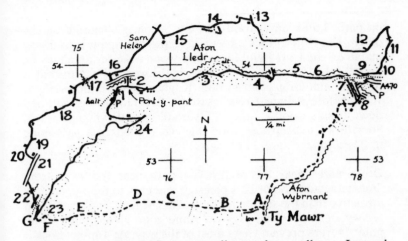

pick up clear track. **14** Ignore smaller track to wall gap. Instead bear R, soon with wall on your L. **15** As track fades keep on to drive on R of house. Turn R along drive and L down track (Sarn Helen). ● **16** After house on L, road bends L. Here go through small gate on R and up field to steps and buildings. Pass just R of house and keep on along track. **17** Go through gate and over stream. Fork R up to large building. Bear slightly L past it. Bear R to pass house on your L. **18** On along lane, soon ignoring a right turn. **19** When lane turns L keep on by following track on R. **20** Go into thicket and at once turn L over stones. Take path over field passing 5 m L of poles. **21** Turn R along road. Turn L along path over bridge. **22** Turn R along track and soon fork L under railway. **23** Turn sharp L along track. **24** After the second open area (recognised by the very winding nature of the track) watch for the track going sharp L down. Follow this back to the start.
Shorter walk. (8.5 km, 5¼ mi, 500 ft) Follow stages 1 to 15. Then carry on down to the main road and L along it.

17A THE LLEDR VALLEY AND TY MAWR

(10 km, 6¼ mi, 1400 ft)

Follow walk 17 stages 1 to 7. Then turn R along track that soon bears R. Soon keep on up lane. **A** 100 m before Ty Mawr go R up path (signed Dolwyddelan) and at once bear L beside wall on your L. Later enter wood. **B** At track go R 10 m along it, then L up path. Later leave wood. **C** Path becomes vague at marshy patch. Keep on to rocky area where the drier path runs above marsh on the L. **D** Before reaching wood a wetter area may be found. If bad, detour 50 m R to avoid the worst of it; cross fallen wall and aim for gate into wood. **E** Ignore small path forking L 100 m before main path reaches wood edge. Go through gate and down beside wood to stile. **F** Over stile and down grass track. Soon fork L to keep near wood edge. **G** At good track go R along it. Then follow stage 24 of walk 17.

Other paths near this walk. The path near the river from Dolwyddelan to point 22 is pleasant and easy to follow, but less attractive than the section in this walk. The high level track from Dolwyddelan to point 23 gives some good views, but E from point 24 trees prevent views most of the way. At Tan-aeldroch it is easy to go SE up to the high level track, but hard to find the rather overgrown path N towards Cwm-celyn. The 3 public paths leaving walk 17A between 772 528 and point E seem to have gone. So has the one from 747 536 to 739 529. The path from Dolwyddelan to Penmachno starts well but becomes vague (and often wet) around Bwlch y Groes. Not recommended.

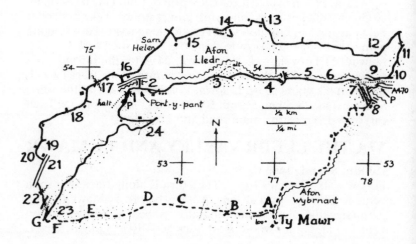

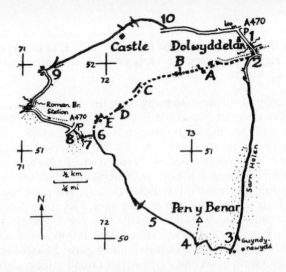

18 DOLWYDDELAN AND ITS CASTLE

(9 km, 5¾ mi, 1100 ft). Map 115, C.

Summary. The longer walk starts by going S along Sarn Helen, a Roman road, along a narrow wooded valley in which the Afon Cwmpenamen flows. Then a forest climb brings you out of the valley into high open country with extensive views that include Snowdon and Moel Siabod. A short detour to Pen y Benar gives good views in other directions. Views continue all the way down. The Afon Lledr is crossed, but, in spite of the station's name, there are no Roman or ancient bridges here. Then a gentle climb through farmland brings the castle into view. This late 12th century Welsh castle, strategically placed in such a splendid setting is well worth a visit. You return along the road with no pavement (but a small verge) for the first 200 m. The 16th century village church contains much of interest, including a lovely carved oak screen and 6th century bronze bell. The shorter walk makes use of an ancient route paved with stone slabs. This attractive path among scattered trees has good views and later rejoins the longer walk. Paths are mainly dry, but can be wet in stages 4 and 5. Usually the stone slabs keep stage B largely mud-free after rain.

Park in the side road near the church (736 523) at Dolwyddelan. Trains stop on request at Dolwyddelan and Roman Bridge stations.

1 Walk along the side road away from the A470. Cross the river and railway and at once turn R along road. **2** Soon fork L up road. **3** After passing the turning to Gwyndy-newydd, turn R up a gap in the forest opposite Tan-y-bwlch. At top of gap go R 10 m, then L up winding track. **4** At top go over stile and on 10 m over bank, then turn R to bottom of slight dip. Here turn L down path (or first go on to explore Pen y Benar). The path becomes a faint grass track keeping R of marshy area. **5** Keep on down when track becomes vague. Make for stile in fence. Soon after this a clear track is joined. **6** When houses are 100 m ahead and you have just passed a rushy area turn L down grass. **7** Go through the middle of 3 farm gates and down path to small bridge. Cross this and turn R along vague path by stream until road is reached. (If overgrown keep on over bridge and turn R down track.) **8** Go on over road and along lane. Later cross river. **9** At farm turn R up track. Keep on along grass track (at first by fence) when track bears L. **10** Keep on along road.

18A A SHORTER VERSION

(7 km, 4¼ mi, 400 ft)
Follow stage 1, then stay by railway (at first) and bear gently L up drive to house. **A** On past house (on R) and barn on your L. On along waymarked path. **B** On over stile and along paved path. **C** When this ends, follow path with wall on your R. **D** On along good track. **E** At farm, track turns R then L through gate. Go up and slightly L over field. **6** Just before a rushy patch (50 m before trees are reached) turn two thirds R down grass. Now follow stage 7 onwards.

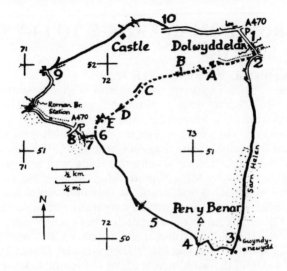

Dolwyddelan Castle

19 FROM ROMAN BRIDGE TO LLYNNAU DIWAUNYDD

(10 km, 6¼ mi, 800 ft) Map 115, C, S.

Summary. After an attractive lowland start across the Lledr valley, you climb gently through plantations. There are unplanted areas, so views can often be enjoyed and you do not feel enclosed. The effort is seen to be well worth it on reaching Llynnau Diwaunydd. The crags of Carnedd y Cribau rise steeply behind the water making a beautiful scene with a ridge on the right gently rising to Moel Siabod. After an indistinct moorland section, a mainly good track is reached after crossing a footbridge. This becomes an easy pleasant return to the rural area. There may be some wet patches between points 3 and 7, also from 10 to 13. For a quicker and dry return, stay on the forest road at 9 and turn L on reaching the minor road. (Saves 2 km, 1¼ mi.) To extend the walk turn R along the minor road at 15 and later go L under the railway. In about 2 km (1 mi) waterfalls and an old clapper bridge are reached. Return the same way.

Park at the junction of the A 470 with the minor road to Roman Bridge Station (716 513) or near Roman Bridge. Trains stop on request.

1 Go along the minor road. **2** Just after crossing over the river, go on along paved path in field, soon bearing L. **3** At road, go on along it 50 m, then R through first gate and up track. For a while there is a wall on your L. **4** On along path when track bends R. **5** Bear L over stream to stile. On up path to reach an open grassy strip between plantations. **6** On along this strip. Follow yellow markers, later crossing a track. **7** Go R along forest road to Llynnau Diwaunydd. (You may like to explore the path along its E side.) **8** Go back along road to where you joined it. **9** Here turn R down path 200 m to stile in fence at forest edge. **10** After a stream crossing (on large slabs) and paved section, the path becomes vague in places. Go roughly W, watching for red-marked posts and tree on skyline. You climb gently and pass 15 m R of this tree. Then make for ruin on R of a group of pines. **11** Just before ruin turn L between stream and pines. Posts show you where to cross stream (100 m past pines). Then follow path SE to bridge. **12** Over bridge and up path soon bearing L to pass

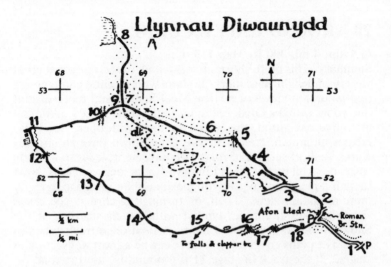

Llynnau Diwaunydd

just R of ruin. **13** On through gate 40 m to marker post (Vague path). Soon a clear track contours round the hill past a few trees. Later it winds down as a sunken grassy or reedy track. **14** On through gate down track. Go half L through farm along drive. **15** Cross road and take paved path over field soon rising to pass just R of pool and on down field to wood bridge. **16** Over bridge and fence and half L over stone slab and second wood bridge. **17** Here go two thirds L along path to follow track over railway bridge which then turns L. **18** On through farm.

Other paths near this walk. The bridleway going W from point 11 is rough and often wet. The road SW from Blaenau Dolwyddelan carries on as a track which passes under the railway (at 691 506) and climbs to the Crimea Pass. It is not suitable for a circular walk as the A470 is too busy to use.

20 AROUND CAPEL CURIG

(6.5 km, 4 mi, 300 ft) Map 115, C.

Summary. This quite short and easy walk reveals to you a great variety of delightful scenery. It starts with a gentle climb giving fine mountain views of nearby Moel Siabod and more distant Snowdon, with the Glyderau range to the right of these. After an attractive oak wood, the walk continues with open views and crosses mountain streams before going down through another wood. A short section of road with pavement, leads to a lovely riverside stroll by the Afon Llugwy with its rocks and falls. Next there is a pine wood where you mostly walk on its edge to enjoy more mountain views. Then, on turning the corner, you reach the twin lakes Llynnau Mymbyr with the classic view of the Snowdon horseshoe behind them. A final open track gets you back. The paths are good, but there can be a short wet section in stage 2. If the track in stage 11 is too muddy, use the road.

Park at Capel Curig car park off minor turning past loos (721 581).

1 Cross road junction, go over stile and up hill. **2** On through wall gap to small gate into wood. **3** Through next small gate. Just after wall gap fork R along smaller path to double slab bridge. Go R over bridge, then follow fence on L to reach a track at entrance gate of house. **4** Here go half R along track. Later go L up fainter track at junction. At tree turn R along path to wood. **5** Follow path through wood, later forking R down to road. Turn L along road. **6** Turn R along minor road over bridge for 50 m. Then turn R again along track for 50 m. Here fork R. **7** Opposite house turn R over stream and go on by river. **8** Turn sharp L just before footbridge is seen. Follow path now high above river. Down steps and along track. **9** Keep on at track junction and fork R after 50 m. **10** On past house and soon R over bridge. **11** Turn L along road. Soon go half R over stile and along track that gently bears R through old wall. **12** Pass just L of house, bear R to gate and R along track.

Other paths near this walk. If you have time in hand turn L along track in stage 12, soon to enjoy new mountain views. A good route runs SW from 734 571 to Llyn y Foel. See walk on p 95. The path'N from near Capel Curig to Llyn Cowlyd is often wet, with boggy patches, and lacks interest. Stiles high above the gate in stage 2 allow you to climb the inviting Clogwyn-mawr, but the route up the ridge to Crimpiau is stopped by a fence near Llyn Coryn.

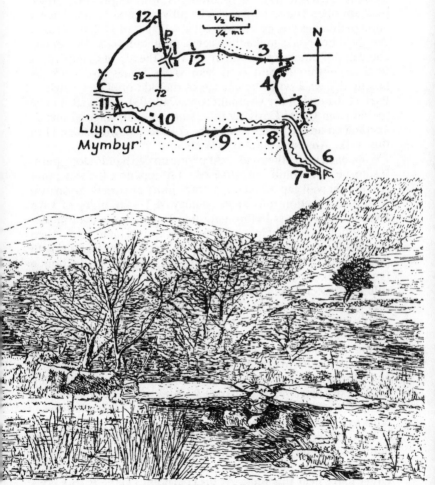

The Double Slab Bridge above Capel Curig

21 SOUTH FROM LLYN CRAFNANT

(10 km, 6¼ mi, 900 ft). Map 115, C.

Summary. A climb up an ancient path in trees brings you to a little known open track leading to the remote, attractive Llyn Bychan. After a walk in plantations with impressive crags, pleasant open country is reached with very good views. Then a good path takes you gently to a col at a height of 1108 ft. Nearby craggy minor peaks make this seem a mountain walk. In fact you could at this point explore the route W to the top of Crimpiau. A final delightful descent with lake views brings you back. A largely dry walk with the chance of the odd brief wet patch.

Park at the end of the Crafnant road (740 603). The walk can be joined from Capel Curig by following walk 20, stages 1 and 2, keeping on up the valley side to the col and following stage 11 of this walk. An extra 3 km or 1¾ mi.

1 Walk back along the road. **2** At phone box go half R along path. It soon bears R uphill and into forest. (At top, note the viewpoint just R after wall gap.) **2** At forest track junction turn R. Soon turn R at next junction into open country. **4** To see more of Llyn Bychan, turn R just before gate into forest and L over ladder stile; follow L edge of lake until path on L rises up to track, then turn R along track. Otherwise stay on track, soon forking R to pass by lake. **5** Ignore L turn but turn sharp R at next junction. **6** Ignore track turning off R. At end of track go on to cross over stile and descend rough track. **7** When grass track goes L through wall gap, turn R over field (NNE) to gate. Over stream and up small steep path that soon bears R, crosses short length of low wall and then runs near another old wall on your L. **8** Soon after seeing ruins ahead, path crosses to other side of wall. Turn L on faint path just before old wall junction. Turn L along track, soon going through wall gap. Carry on down (WSW) to vague crossing track 50 m before reaching a tree. **9** Here turn R along level path with wet hollow on its L. Aim between 2 tree-covered hillocks, cross a clearer path and pass 2 post-like stumps. **10** On past group of rocks down to clear path and R along it. **11** At col fork L down path. **12** Go through gate in wall and towards house, soon bearing R down field to road.

Other paths near this walk. At the col (point 11) the R fork goes down steeply at 2 places, passing through woods to reach road at 746 605.

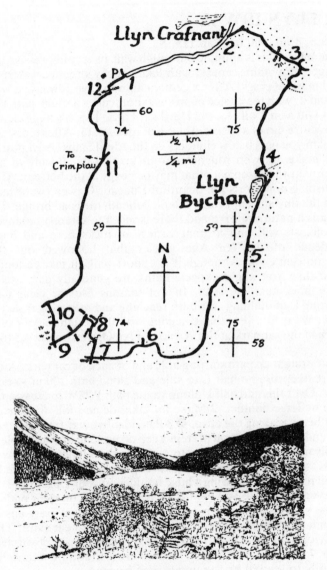

Llyn Crafnant

22 LLYN IDWAL

(5 km, 3 mi, 900 ft) Map 115, S.

Summary. This is a simple but rough walk in very impressive and rugged mountain scenery, with lakes, rocky streams, waterfalls and massive crags. After a gentle climb to Llyn Idwal you walk round it, with the choice of an easy short cut or a rough path that gets you near Twll Du, the Devil's Kichen. This is a huge cleft in the centre dip of a splendid curve of rock strata. After crossing a stream you pass below climbers on the Idwal Slabs. Adventurers can make an even rougher detour up to Llyn Bochlwyd and return down a steep path that may be boggy at the bottom. After returning don't miss the beautiful Rhaeadr Ogwen (waterfalls) and the tiny ancient bridge rebuilt beneath the road bridge. The area is a nature reserve and there is much to interest botanists. Geologists will find a great variety of rocks here and much evidence of the Ice Age glacier that hollowed out this magnificent cwm. Although it is a short walk, it takes a longer time than you might expect. Paths are generally dry, except sometimes near the start. In wet seasons use the clear path starting L of buildings for both reaching and returning from the lake. Wear footwear that can cope with the rough rocky paths. **Park** in the car park at the W end of Llyn Ogwen on the A5 (649 604).

1 Go straight up path starting at R end of back of car park. After short steep rise go half L to stile and along path 100 m to next stile. Over this and half L along vague path W/SW to cross small stile by large boulder. **2** Make for lakeside and follow the path that bears L along the edge. ● **3** Path climbs away from lake. At the end of a long section of steps keep on up 15 m and scramble R easily up rocks to join more steps. **4** By a short length of low wall on R, turn half L along nearly level path lined on each side by small rocks. After passing a huge boulder on your L pass just L of an even larger one and bear R by it. Here go L on clear path. **5** Cross waterfall. (If this is too tricky, turn L down grass beside stream. At bottom, cross flat area to join path near cairn. This soon joins the main path.) ● **6** Through gate and back down clear path. **7** Go down A5 200 m to layby. Turn L to admire waterfalls. Turn R to see old bridge under road bridge.

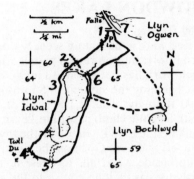

Short cut. After stages 1 and 2, follow path as it climbs away from lakeside. Just before it crosses stream on a stone slab, turn L by stream. Turn R over stream when opposite large boulder on your L. Soon join path which crosses second stream. Go over flat area keeping R of rushes, to join path near cairn. This rejoins main path round lake. Now follow stages 6 and 7.

Extension. Follow stages 1 to 5. Just before wall (200 m before end of lake) turn R beside it. At top keep on (path at times) to Llyn Bochlwyd. Here turn L down path.

Other paths near this walk. The path along the N edge of Llyn Ogwen is in many places hard to trace and often has wet stretches.

23 THE SNOWDON LAKES

(8 km, 5 mi, 1000 ft) Map 115, S.

Summary. This fine walk in mountain scenery does not involve too much upward effort, but the return path is rough in places, even though much work has been done to improve it. You also have the option of gaining the summit of Snowdon (this adds 4 km, 2½ mi, 1500 ft to the walk). The walk starts along the Miners' Track with a gentle climb past Llyn Teyrn to go across a causeway and walk beside Llyn Llydaw with the towering cliffs of Y Lliwedd on the left and Crib Goch on the right. Rather more effort gets you up beside waterfalls to Glaslyn, the lake from which Afon Glaslyn starts its long course to the sea. Soon you reach the Pig Track, with splendid views down to Llyn Llydaw and later of Llanberis Pass.

Park (only free out of season) at the top of Llanberis Pass (648 556) or get there by Sherpa bus.

1 From car park go along nearly level track S. **2** Near second lake fork R, soon crossing causeway. **3** As you bear R by third lake and then start bearing L, turn R up small path in grass. Keep on up if it fades, soon reaching Pig track. (To reach Snowdon, turn L along it and L again at top of zig-zags.) Bear R along this path. **4** At col go on down clear path. **5** Through wall gap to car park.

Other paths near this walk. A path runs SE from the top of the pass to the power station (653 540). Apart from wet patches, it is quite good but not useful for circular walks.

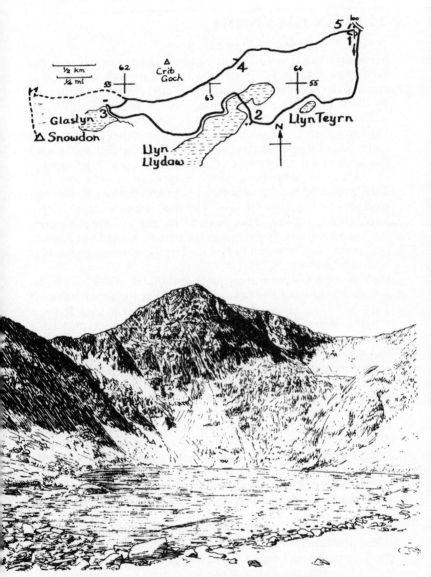

Snowdon's summit towers over the blue waters of Glaslyn

24 LLYN GWYNANT

(12 km, 7½ mi, 900 ft) Map 115, S.

Summary. This fine walk is little known and can be shortened at both ends of the lake. It starts with an easy ascent with good views of the lake and, in May or June, attractive rhododendrons by the path. After passing through dense pines an easy open section takes you over an attractive stream and down a lane looking towards Snowdon. After short stretches of woodland and road (with pavement) you join an attractive path well above the back of Llyn Gwynant. A spectacular rock outcrop here makes a good picnic place with a very steep drop to the lake. Then attractive natural woodland is passed through before the path runs by the Afon Glaslyn. The final return is mainly down an old lane with lovely views down to the lake. After wet weather there are a few muddy patches in the pinewood, and wet patches near point 5 and between 14 and 15. The worst patch (avoidable) is on the short cut N.

Park by Llyn Gwynant near its N end on the A498 (648 518). **1** Walk by the road SW towards Beddgelert for about 300 m. **2** Turn half L up signposted stony track. When it goes R keep straight on beside rhododendrons. **3** After keeping on past a bend in the track rejoin it higher up. **4** Turn R to barn when wall on your R ends. Just before barn, go L along track. Soon go half L off track along path near wall on your L. The path turns R in pines, and runs by another wall for a while. **5** On out of wood. Soon go through small iron gate, over plank bridge and up a slight rise, slowly moving away from wall on your R. **6** Go through wall gap. Soon path runs between 2 lines of poles. **7** Over bridge and on to lane. Here go R. **8** When road starts to bend L and gently rises, fork R down path at footpath sign. After bridge, turn L along drive. **9** 30 m before gate across track fork R over stile and along path in trees. **10** R along road. **11** L down through small gate 50 m before house on L. Bear L over field to cross bridge. **12** Turn R beside river for 50 m. Then go on by grassy bank on your L. Later go on with wall and trees just on your R. **13** When wall bears R make for gap in wall ahead. Through gap and half L up path over heap of rust-coloured stones to tree at bend in wall. **14** Soon go through wall gap and fence gap, then down path towards lake and group of pines. **15** Cross bridge just L of large

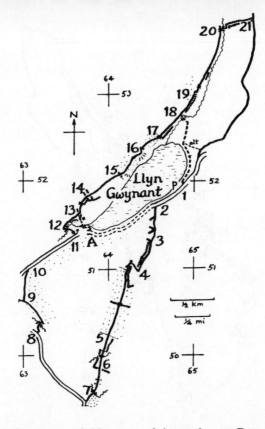

outcrop and enter wood. Near top of rise path goes R and almost at once L. Soon a fine viewpoint is reached with a sharp drop down to the lake. **16** Here carry on down clear path with steps. It stays high until near the end of the lake. **17** After descent go over stile and on to bridge. ● **18** Do not cross bridge. Keep on for 300 m by fence to stile. **19** Here go R over it and at once L. Soon on over second stile. Follow path by old wall. **20** When 200 m from power station cross stile and turn R over bridge. Turn L and soon R to follow path by wall. **21** At lane go R down it to road and down road to starting point.

73

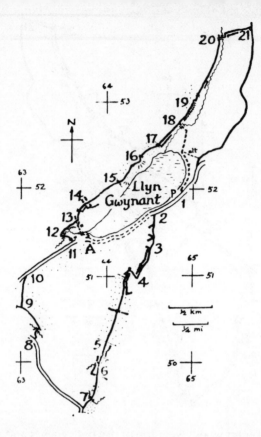

24A SHORT CUT SOUTH

making walk 7.5 km, 4½ mi, 500 ft.
1 Walk by the road SW towards Beddgelert. **A** Just after lake ends go through wall gap down steps and sharp L to cross bridge. On past house and through wall gap to track. On along track 20 m then go R through wall gap and L to another gap. Then bear R to heap of rust-coloured stones and to tree at bend in wall. Now follow instruction 14 etc.

24B SHORT CUT NORTH

making walk 9.5 km, 6 mi, 700 ft.
Follow main walk to stage 17 and go R over bridge. **B** Go half R over field to small gate near lake side. This leads to a path over a tiny hill overlooking lake. The last part by the lake is often wet, in which case the road can be reached using a track L of the above 'small gate'.
A walk round the lake (4.5 km, 2¾ mi, 300 ft) is obtained by making both short cuts.
Other paths near this walk. The path E from footbridge 649 527 has been diverted to reach the lane at 654 525. It is easy to extend the walk N to the power station 653 540. There are no public routes W from Llyn Gwynant to the Watkin path. For a Watkin path walk see p.101.

25 FROM NANMOR TO LLYN DINAS

(12.5 km, 7¾ mi, 1500 ft) Map 115, S, H.
Summary. This walk starts with a gentle climb up Cwm Bychan, soon with extensive views. At the top fine new views towards Snowdon are seen, and later the perfect setting of Llyn Dinas is enjoyed with hills surrounding it on all sides. In August heather enriches the scene. Next comes a gentle climb away from the lake through a pleasant wood and then rhododendron country to Hafod-Owen, a remote cottage. Soon a tiny road is used until you reach footpaths that run pleasantly through short lengths of deciduous woods before the final return through fields. After rain there can be short wet patches here and there, the worst likely to be in stage 10.
Park in the Nanmor car park (597 462) on the A4085 E of Aberglaslyn Pass. The walk can also be started from the layby on the A498 just SW of Llyn Dinas (612 494).

1 At the car park walk up (keeping L of loos) to the bed of the old railway. Cross it near the tunnel entrance and go on up the path with the stream below on your R. Follow path all the way up the valley to the top. **2** Here turn L along level path to the next junction, at which there is an old mine on your L. **3** Here go sharp R down stony path that soon bears L. **4** Follow zig-zag path nearly to bridge. Then turn sharp R along lakeside path. **5** Through gate and up path bearing away from lake. **6** Go down past ruin (on your R) to path along wood edge. **7** By cairn at top of small rise, go half R over low wall and up path. Soon go on through low wall gap. Then through another wall gap and turn half L beside this low wall for a while. **8** Path leaves wood and soon crosses stream. Follow path on. **9** After a short steep descent and a rise you come to wall gap. Here go on 10 m then half L up path. **10** Over stile and half R up through thicket. **11** Pass just L of house and go down by wall by your L. **12** Over stile just L of larches and half R by wall down to track and on. **13** Cross wall by stile and carry on with wall now on your L. After a short steep rise, path veers L, then R to road. **14** Turn R along road. **15** Soon after track on R go half R over stiles and follow posts across field to join path, soon with stream on your L. **16** After stile, pass just L of house. **17** Go through small gate and on (gently up at first). **18** Pass just L of next house. After 100 m go on up in wood, then down zig-zag path. **19** Go on past path junction, with wall on your R. Cross stone step in wall, turn R over stile and L through small gate. Soon join clear track. **20** Soon after track bears R and climbs, you reach a field on the L. Here leave track and bear L across field to go through gate near pole. **21** Follow wall on your R. Go through wall gap and up to the R hand of two farm gates. **22** Cross farmyard and go half L down lane. **23** After gate across road, turn R through wall gap beside house. Follow markers down to bottom corner of field. **24** Here go on 70 m to small gate and diagonally over field to bridge. Then bear slightly L (passing L of outcrop) to reach drive and go along it. **25** Turn R back along road.

Other paths near this walk. The N section of the path over Bwlch y Battel (637 469) is good but S of the pass it becomes vague and wet. The path S from 618 460 has gone, and the area is mainly wet or tussocky grass. The path S of Llyn Dinas can easily be

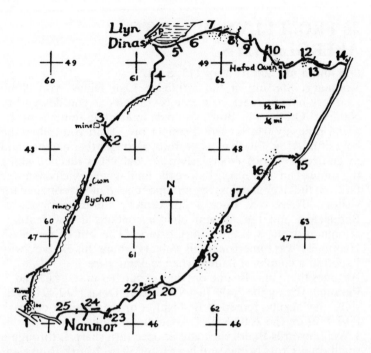

followed to the road at 627 502 but a circuit of the lake involves road walking without pavement. (In places you can walk on the low flat wall.) The track N from 631 490 is good. The path starting at 637 494 (which is wrongly drawn on the 2½ inch map) soon follows the Afon Llynedno up to the lake. There are wet stretches. Adventurers can then reach the ridge and go S and later SW to rejoin a return path near Llyn yr Adar, which also has wet sections.

A simple railway walk can be made by following stage 1, but turning R near tunnel. After crossing minor and main road it soon runs just R of farm track. After crossing a small river, turn sharp L along lane (601 435). Go on over cross-road and sharp L back at the next junction. Distance 7 km, 4½ mi. At this last junction there is a chance to explore an interesting ancient track sharp R up into the hills. (Can be wet near start.)

26 FROM LLYN DINAS TO ABERGLASLYN

(9.5 km, 6 mi, 800 ft) Map 115, S, H.

Summary. Starting at the attractive Llyn Dinas, you climb heathery hills to reach new extensive views as you descend to Nanmor. On the way down you pass interesting remains of the aerial ropeway which carried copper ore. Then you follow the beautiful Afon Glaslyn as it runs through the narrow and magnificent Pass of Aberglaslyn. Beddgelert is reached along the route of an old railway before the final stages which are never far from the river and pass Sygun copper mine, now reopened for visitors. There was once a 6th century Celtic monastry at Beddgelert and the present church contains a few features remaining from a 12th century priory. 'The Inn of the Sixth Happiness' was filmed near this walk. (Perhaps this explains why I spotted a couple of llamas when walking here.)

At times there may be one or two wet patches in stages 3 and 7.

Park in layby on the A498 just SW of Llyn Dinas (612 494). The walk may also be joined at Beddgelert or the Nanmor car park (597 462) on the A4085 E of Aberglaslyn Pass.

1 Walk towards Beddgelert and at once turn sharp L through a small gate. Cross bridge and bear L for 50 m. **2** Fork R up clear zig-zag path. **3** As gradient eases path bears L up small rocky outcrop. Soon there is a stream on your L. **4** As path starts to rise, take the R stony fork. **5** Keep on through old mine at top, and after 100m, bear L near post and then R. Here a path goes down to a flat grassy area. **6** Here bear L (S) down, passing just L of pool. **7** When there is a hillock ahead, bear L of it and soon join path down valley. **8** Path passes to the R of a boggy patch and then goes through small gate in wall. **9** Cross old railway and keep on roughly level path in trees. **10** Just before river, turn R along path that runs a few m above it. **11** When tunnel is seen up on your R, turn R up boulder path. Then turn L along old railway bed. **12** Near bridge, carry on along the same side of the river (or cross bridge and turn R along the other side). **13** Beside next bridge bear R beside river. **14** Go on past another bridge still with river on your L. **15** At yet another bridge go on along lane. ● **16** At lane end go on along grass path by wall (on your L). Soon

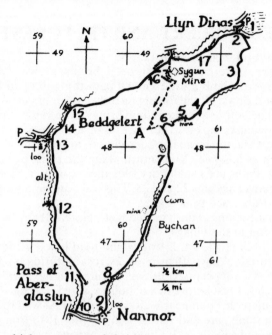

join track which goes towards bridge over river, but turn R along path just before bridge. **17** Make for ladder stile and go on by wall.

A shorter walk starting from Beddgelert (7.5 km, 4½ mi, 800 ft). At the road junction (A498 and A4085) cross bridge and walk E beside river past loos and over footbridge. Follow stages 14 and 15. **16** At lane end fork half R along track to entrance gate to Sygun mine. Here turn R along path just outside fence. It bears L by wall and soon turns sharp R up hillside. (Good views after a while.) **A** Near top follow path sharp L. **6** At top bear R (S) down, passing just L of pool. Now follow stages 7 onwards.

Other paths near this walk. A route with good views starts steeply near the S end of the row of cottages in Beddgelert (592 481). It is not too easy to follow but reaches a gate in the wall, where a good path L brings you to point 6. Vague paths go from this gate to 597 475, then NE to point 6. Paths W of the road between Beddgelert and Pont Aberglaslyn are vague in some places and often have wet stretches.

27 BEDDGELERT AND ITS FOREST

(9km, 5½ mi, 600 ft) Map 115, S.

Summary. After a beautiful stroll beside a river, the Afon Glaslyn, you climb a little known path through open farmland with good views. At the forest you follow the rocky Afon Colwyn for a while before a further climb brings more views, this time of the Snowdon range etc. There are large open areas in this part of the forest and the route has been chosen to keep you in the open as much as possible. You return along the track bed of an old railway. Paths are usually dry, but there can be a short muddy patch between points 22 and 23. This walk can be combined with the next one. See walk 28A.

Park in the main car park in Beddgelert (588 481) by the A498 at the W end of the village.

1 Walk back (E) towards bridge and road junction. Just before bridge turn R along path by river. **2** Cross footbridge and keep on by river. Go on past next bridge. **3** Turn L at next bridge and R along road. **4** Just before row of houses, turn L through farm gate and go up path, soon near wall on your R. **5** At wall junction go through small gate and follow wall on your R to iron gate. Go through and soon bear L along track passing just R of house. **6** On along grass track at a crossing track. **7** Turn R up road and L down forest road over bridge. **8** Soon go R over footbridge and half R along path to river. Turn L beside it. ● **9** The path bears L to follow a stream at wood edge. Soon turn R along track over bridge. At once ignore main track bearing L, and keep on along grassy track. **10** When track bears L and narrows near a stream, leave it and go along L edge of field with stream below on your L. Soon go R along track to wall gap. **11** Here go on (N) over field to barn (100 m from L end of fence). Use the 2 stones to cross fence just R of barn. **12** Go L on track just beyond barn. Soon go over stile and along path in pines. At track turn R along it. ● **13** Keep on at track junction. **14** At the 5-way junction follow the main track bearing L. **15** Ignore track L to house. Soon fork L. Then go R up track in trees. Ignore R fork to house. **16** Go L at track junction. **17** Turn down L at next junction. Soon turn R along track that goes at once over bridge and L. **18** Follow grass path on wood edge (between wall and fence). (If no stile to cross fence,

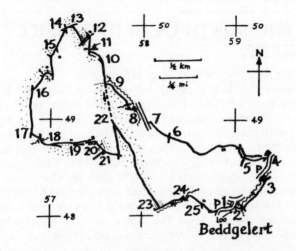

stay on track to end of strip of pines on your L. Then turn L down path with wall on your L and pines R. At wall steps follow stage 21 etc.) **19** At ruin go through wall gap and down field towards house with wall on your R. 100 m before house, go R and at once L down between walls. **20** Just after shed on R, turn R through small gate. Cross stream 50 m R of trees and go on to steps in L end of long wall. **21** Here turn half L along path. At track turn L. **22** At junction turn sharp R along track (old railway). **23** Turn L at T-junction in pines. **24** Go R over second bridge to ladder stile. Follow track by stream. **25** Go through gate on L to pass large concrete 'block' in field. Soon through gate and L down drives to road.

Short version (6 km, 3¾ mi, 300 ft). Follow 1 to 8. **9** The path bears L to follow stream at wood edge. Soon turn L along track for 1.5 km, (1 mi) and follow 23 to 25.

28 THE NORTH OF BEDDGELERT FOREST.

(7.5 km, 4¾ mi, 1000 ft) Map 115, S.

Summary. The map shows this area heavily afforested, but large regions have now been felled giving good views. After climbing by a mountain stream and forest tracks, you reach a fine open view, with the Snowdon range NE. Then an old trackway takes you to the top of the pass, Bwlch-y-ddwy-elor, where a new view down the Pennant valley appears. After a short descent through old mines, a rough path takes you over another pass. Next a section of forest, followed by a fine high level path, during which Llyn Llywelyn, a lake hidden among trees, is seen below you. Again the return down the forest is well broken by open stretches. There can be wet patches at point 6 and between points 8 to 11.

Park at the forest car park (574 502) reached after leaving the A4085 3.5 km (2 mi) N of Beddgelert.

1 Go up path 50 m E of toilets and L along track. **2** Turn R up path just after crossing stream. This path follows stream and crosses it just before reaching track. **3** Here turn L along track and soon sharp R at junction. **4** Go on up rough track at crossroads. **5** Keep on at next junction for 150 m then turn L up path signposted Dolbenmaen. **6** At top go through wall and at once fork L down. (If wet fork R for 50 m then get down to path). **7** Keep on down through mine when curved track comes in on your R. Ignore paths going half R to ruins. At slate heaps follow path as it narrows and bears L to the gap in the ridge on your L. Take care not to fall into mine holes here. **8** At top a wet area can be dodged by keeping close to wall on the L. Go over wall and stile and down into forest. **9** Turn L along track for 80 m then R up path. **10** Leave forest and follow open path. (Blue markers.) **11** Down into forest. **12** Go L along track and at once R down path. Turn R along track and R at next junction. ● **13** Turn sharp L at next track junction. **14** Ignore L turning to house, but soon turn L at junction. **15** Fork R down to a 5-way junction. Here follow main track bearing R. **16** Ignore R turns, cross stream and, at T-junction, turn L back to car park.

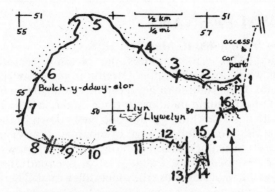

28A A LONGER WALK

(15 km, 9¼ mi, 1300 ft).
Follow stages 1 to 12. Go on past track junction. Then follow walk 27 stages 17 to 25 and 1 to 12. Turn sharp R at track junction and follow walk 28 stage 16.

Other paths near this walk. The path N out of the forest at 558 515 can be wet for the first 400 m. The other path out of the forest from 565 518 to 554 533 (where it is blocked by barbed wire) seems to have gone.

Looking over the forest to the snow-capped Snowdon Range

29 CWM PENNANT

(8.5 km, 5¼ mi, 400 ft) Map 115, H, S.

Summary. This walk explores the pleasant remote valley through which runs the Afon Dwyfor from its source in the mountains of the Nantlle ridge. It can be extended to a 6 mi walk by a visit to old mine buildings further up the valley. The walk starts with a gentle climb giving good views down to the valley. Later on the Moel Hebog range of mountains tower up to the East. The return first uses an old railway bed, with views towards the more wooded areas. Paths West of the road are hard to follow, so the final stages use the quiet valley road. There may be 2 or 3 wet patches after rain.

Parking. Leave the A487 at Dolbenmaen (505 431). Fork L at phone box (531 454). Again fork L to bridge. Just over a mile (1.5 km) further on, park by another bridge (532 476).

1 Go on along road 300 m until it bears L to cross river. Here leave road and keep on along track. Pass just R of barns. **2** When track turns sharp R leave it to go straight on near wall and fence on your L. When you see another fence running up away from this fence, make for a point 50 m up it to go through a small gate. **3** Cross nearly level grass with steeper ground and bracken on your R. (If wet a short detour R will avoid some of the wet area). Watch for an isolated 4 m length of wall; R of this take path in bracken up to a marker post. Here zig-zag up to plantation corner. **4** Through gate. Slant up wettish field to track. **5** Here you can detour L along track to explore mine buildings and get closer mountain views. Otherwise turn R. Ignore two paths on R of track. **6** The track bears L to contour hillside. Detour slightly L if wet here. **7** After several bridges, a wall runs by your R and you reach the deeply cut Afon Cwm-llefrith. Here turn R beside fence. **8** At field bottom go on over two stiles and down faint track. It turns L just after slate bridge over ditch. Pass just L of farm and along road. **9** At phone box go R along road and later fork L back to start.

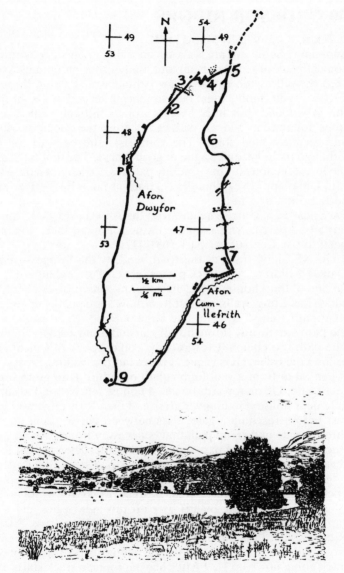

Looking up the Pennant Valley

30 CROESOR RIDGES

(6.5 km, 4 mi, 900 ft) Map 124, H.

Summary. Soon you are walking on a fine open ridge with the conical peak of Cnicht ahead and many other mountains to be seen as well as the estuary view behind you. Passing through Croesor, you climb a quiet lane to reach a second ridge. At first this is wooded, but later becomes open through well spaced trees, followed by a lovely path gently down the side of the ridge and an easy final stage. The route is quite easy to follow, although paths become vague or go in places. The first track and the forest section may have muddy patches. To lengthen the walk turn L at point 7 to explore the old track as far as the bridge. This adds 1.5 km or 1 mi.

Park near Pont Garreg-hylldrem on the A4085 (615 431) 5 km (3 mi) S of Aberglaslyn Pass. As parking is limited there you may need to use Croesor car park (631 447).

1 Go NE along track at the road bend by the bridge — Pont Garreg-hylldrem. The track passes just L of second house. **2** At far end of third house turn L up slope, passing just R of boulder which has 2 tiny 'walls' against it. Follow vague paths up to join clear path going L to get round large outcrop. Near wall follow the path's U-turn R through wall gap and along top of outcrop. The path soon bears R towards the conical peak of Cnicht and follows the ridge. (It is vague at times but the walking is easy.) **3** When 80 m from a wall follow path one third L to go through small gate. Go on towards house. **4** Follow fence round to small gate near house. Go on over grass and turn R through wall gap just before reaching a gate. Pass between barns. Soon turn L through gate and go up path that bears away from wall. Stay on 'shelf' above wall and pass shed by holly tree. Then go half R to regain the open ridge. **5** Cross wall by stone steps slightly R of ridge crest. Keep on towards Cnicht. Soon bear L to keep on open ground between two areas of trees. Make for white house (slightly L of straight ahead) by path through rushes and wall gap. **6** Go through fence gap near house and along drive. **7** Turn R down lane. Pass the Croesor car park and continue SE over crossroads. **8** At top of rise turn R along forest track. Ignore track going down on L. **9** After leaving forest a track starts at a house. 100 m further on go one third R up path to small gate in

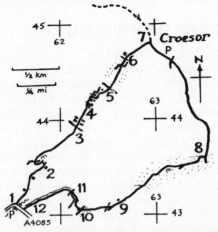

wall. Follow path down into wood. **10** R along road, soon L through gate and half R down field. Bear R along bottom fence and follow fence as it turns L. **11** Go through gate, over track and over stile. Keep on along bank with ditch on your R. **12** Turn R along road.

Other paths near this walk. The second ridge can be followed down further than is done in this walk, but trees greatly restrict the views.

Looking back to Cnicht while descending ridge

31 LLANFROTHEN TO RHYD

(9.5 km, 5¾ mi, 500 ft) Map 124, H.

Summary. The walk starts along a quiet lane and over fields to the tiny isolated village of Llanfrothen, with its small restored medieval church. As you gently climb through attractively wooded but mainly open country, fine mountain views are seen, the nearest being Moelwyn Bach, Moelwyn Mawr and the Cnicht ridge. Route finding here needs some care; it can be avoided in the shorter version. Near Rhyd you turn back to enjoy views of the estuary and sea, which are then lost for a while in pinewoods. The final stage runs near the Ffestiniog railway as it descends to Penrhyndeudraeth. At times there maybe a few wet patches.

Park by the A4085 (615 400) 200 m past the first bend after the long straight mile (1.5 km) S from Garreg.

1 Go NE to road bend and fork R along lane. **2** After passing wood on your L, turn L along drive which soon turns R. Ignore L turn to Fron-oleu. **3** When drive turns L keep on through gate over field with fence on your R. **4** Cross footbridge and go L beside stream 50 m to stone slabs over smaller stream. Follow path towards church with hedge on your R. (Use field on R if path is too muddy.) **5** Turn L at far corner of house on your L and follow path to grassy area. Near churchyard gate bear R between 2 houses. ● **6** Turn L along lane. **7** Cross road and go down path to bridge. Pass just R of chapel and at once turn L then R between buildings. **8** Through gate, bearing L with path to stile. Go on over stile along path which bears R to run NE. **9** At stream bear R 70 m to cross stile. Go up field by fence on your L to gate. Here go R along drive. **10** Fork L up drive. Soon fork L again. **11** At crossroad turn R to house and R through small gate. Go down field by wall and make for gate 60 m away from wall. **12** Through gate. Bear L down field to gate L of house in trees. Here go on 30 m to next gate but don't go through. Go into field just R of gate and follow green track. It later bears away from fence into rushy area. **13** Here fork one third L 50 m along path to group of willows, then go R to stone slab bridge. Join clear path to pass just L of ruin, and at once turn two thirds L up path in bracken. Down with wall on L. **14** Go half R over level ground to small wall gap just R of rocky tree-covered knoll. Here go on (at right angles to wall) to join a vague track. It soon reaches a clear track

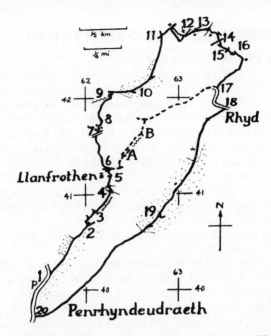

at a point just R of a much larger rocky tree-covered knoll. Turn
L (SE) along this track. **15** When track becomes vague keep on to
cross over another vague one. Descend quite steeply towards
house. **16** Cross stile in fence and bear L to join grass track to
house. At house go R along track. **17** Turn L along road. **18** Near
road sign 'Rhyd' turn sharp R along grass track. Go through gate
and turn half L. If wet patch is met detour L by fence. Soon enter
forest. **19** Fork R along level track. Soon on out of forest. **20** Turn
R along road.

Shorter walk avoiding vague paths. (7.5 km, 4¾ mi, 500 ft)
Follow stages 1 to 5. **6** Turn R along lane, and soon L along drive
to Maes Gwyr Lleyn. **A** Cross stile just L of house, then go R by
fence and later by stream. **B** On along track. Turn R at road.
Follow stages 18 to 20.

Other paths near this walk. The pleasant route N from 623 421
becomes difficult after 0.5 km. I could not find the paths near
Rhyd that go SE from 637 423 and W from 633 419, or the ones on
the R of the walk at 630 411 and 622 405.

32 NORTH WEST OF FFESTINIOG

(6.5 km, 4 mi, 700 ft) Map 124, H.

Summary. At first an attractive stream — the Afon Teigl — is followed. Then a gentle climb across open country reaches splendid views of the Moelwyn mountains. Next the elusive Afon Goedol, which runs mainly through woods, is met several times, and two of its fine waterfalls are seen. For a while the path runs in dense pines, but soon the scene becomes more open and delightful natural woods are seen during the final mile. The paths are largely clear and usually dry. (Perhaps a wet patch in stage 8.) The walk can be combined with the Coedydd Maentwrog walk 33 using the link described, making a total of 16 km, 10 mi, 1800 ft. (May be wet patches near start of link.)

Park by the bridge at Rhyd-y-sarn (691 422) on the A496 5 km (3 mi) S of Blaenau Ffestiniog.

1 Walk S (away from B. Ffestiniog) from the car park and soon turn sharp L up drive. **2** When drive bears R to house keep on along grassy track. **3** Just after barn at wood corner, turn L down field to bridge. Cross it and turn L along path to next bridge. Just before bridge, turn sharp R up path. **4** Later path climbs a tiny ridge. Turn R up steps and ignore the smaller path going on. On leaving wood, follow the rocky stream below you on the R. **5** Turn L up track. **6** When drive turns R keep on down grass. Over bridge, over road and on to next road. **7** Here turn half L up field (by low bank). Down through wall gap near barn. Just past barn bear R along beside wall (kept on your R). **8** Go through wall where it turns L and follow it down to road. Turn R along road. Ignore first bridge. **9** Turn L down signposted track over next bridge. **10** Just after house cross small slate bridge and follow dark path in pine wood. **11** After passing to the L of a shed, turn L at junction down over bridge (waterfall here). 50 m after bridge go on through gate, soon reaching track and turning sharp R along it. **12** 20 m before ruin, turn L through wall gap to barn. Follow clear path just R of barn, soon with wall on your R. **13** At junction turn R down path with wall on your L. ● **14** At river turn L through gate, L a few m and R along path with wall on your R. Turn R along road.

Link with walk 33: Follow stages 1 to 13. **14** At river turn R to cross bridge. Then L by river, soon bearing R and climbing away

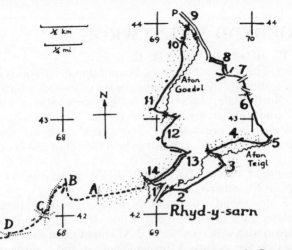

from river. **A** Keep on out of dense pine wood. On meeting a track, go up it. **B** After passing a wall on the L, turn sharp L up stony path, soon by railway. Follow footpath signs through the station. **C** At far end of station go R over stile and L by railway and under bridge. Follow path about 20 m from railway, keeping L of some low outcrops. **D** Cross railway and turn R down to track. Go down track and follow walk 33 stage 6 etc.

Other paths near this walk. I found no bridge at point 5. The paths N of point 8 are hard to follow. The path through 680 420 seems to have gone.

Above the Ffestiniog Railway on the link between Walks 32 and 33

33 COEDYDD MAENTWROG

(5 km, 3¼ mi, 600 ft) Map 124, H.

Summary. This walk explores the beautiful natural woods in the Vale of Ffestiniog. These are a relict of the oakwoods which once covered North Wales. Most of the walk follows paths well above the valley bottom, giving fine views on the open stretches. The paths are clear and normally dry. See walk 32 for an extension of this walk. It is also worth exploring the nature trail just N of Llyn Mair.

Park near the E end of Llyn Mair (654 413) on the B4410 1.5 km (1 mi) from Maentwrog.

1 Walk E along road towards Maentwrog. Just after it bends R, turn L along track in forest. Later ignore track turning R down, and keep on with wall on your R. **2** At end of plantation on your R, go on over fence, turn R through wall gap and L along gently rising path. Soon ignore path going steeply down under cables. **3** Go on over bridge and up, to walk beside railway. **4** When railway bears L, the path bears R keeping near fence on your L. Later the path goes down to cross stream and rises up to pass through wall gap. **5** Go down to house and sharp R down track. **6** At sharp bend, go over stile and down path over bridge with waterfall on your R. **7** Go through gate and down rough zig-zag path to clear track. Here turn R along track past house, over bridge and through gate. **8** Where path gets near wall turn R up path. **9** At path junction near stile on R and pines, go L down path. It later passes R of house and over small bridge. **10** Path bears L down to track. Go on along track and then on up road.

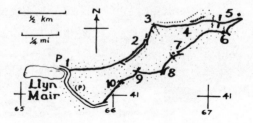

34 SOUTH OF FFESTINIOG

(5 km, 3 mi, 500 ft) Map 124, H.

Summary. After passing through a lovely wood you gently climb a splendid ridge with views of the Vale of Ffestiniog and the Moelwyn mountains. At the village of Ffestiniog you follow a good open route to see Rhaeadr Cynfal — impressive waterfalls contained within a narrow rocky gorge. A path high on the south bank of the stream takes you back down into another attractive wood — apart from a dark 5 minutes among pines. Paths are generally good, but there is one small field which is often muddy.

Park along the minor road at the junction of the A496 and B4391 (687 416) 1.5 km (1 mi) E of Ffestiniog. Or park in Ffestiniog and join walk at point 6 (signposted to the falls).

1 Go back to the major road junction, fork R up road and soon turn R up track in wood. **2** Fork L 100 m before wood edge. Over stile and on by wall on your L. **3** At wall junction follow wall uphill, keeping it on your R. **4** Follow faint grass track that bends L then R near pylon. It is now about 15 m from wall. **5** Turn R up road. **6** At the second footpath sign turn R down through farm. Go through gate and down field aiming just L of pines. **7** When stile and bridge are seen, bear L to cross them. Follow path up through gate. **8** Over steps in wall. Bear R through gate into field and follow grass track. **9** After stile fork R down to falls. Follow path above stream to bridge. **10** Cross bridge, climb steps and turn R along path near wood edge. **11** Through small gate, over stream and on by wall for 50 m. Then go through wall gap and bear L by wall to join clear wide path down open hillside. **12** Keep on to stile when path stops (or turns sharp R). Over stile and down muddy field to gate. Down rough track (later it narrows). **13** On into wood. **14** Turn R along road.

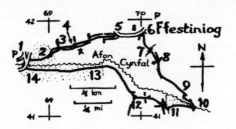

35 CWM CYNFAL

(7 km, 4½ mi, 600 ft) Map 124, B.

Summary. After glimpses of Llyn Morynion ('Lake of the Maidens') a broad ridge is descended with good views including the Moelwyn mountains. The return starts in the attractive valley beside the Afon Cynfal. The climax is reached as the path climbs out of the spectacular cwm with its fine waterfall — Rhaeadr-y-cwm. Paths are usually good, but one patch could be wet in stage 14.

Park by the S edge of Llyn Dubach (746 424) by the B4407, 0.5 km (¼ mi) N of the junction with the B4391, 5 km (3 mi) E from Ffestiniog. Or park by Pont Newydd on A470 (714 409) and walk NE along minor road to join walk at point 10.

1 Go along track which bears L to a gate. Go through and on at 45° to fence over grass. (To see more of the lake when it comes into view, bear R over grass dodging marshy areas to join edge path.) **2** Pass just R of marshy area, now along grass track towards line of poles. **3** Go on under poles to join clear stony track by wall on its L. It bears R then (near lake) L. **4** Take L fork towards road, with wall near your L. **5** Turn R down road. **6** After going down towards bend sign, turn L along clear track. **7** When track turns L keep straight on along grass path. Through wall gap and on with wall on your R. **8** Cross low fence, now with fence and wall on your R. After 100 m at fence gap go half L down field to wall gap beside ruin. **9** Keep on beside old sunken track. The track is later raised up. Join it and carry on through farm to road. **10** Turn L along road. **11** Ignore track forking R down to bridge. **12** At Cwm Farm keep on along field edge with wall on your R. **13** Over ladder stile and L up steep path. **14** At a marshy patch path bears R, soon with old wall or fence on the R. (If wet, detour to the L.) At top, cross fence for precipitous view down ravine. **15** As path becomes vague bear L to walk near road and join road at gate. **16** Turn L at road junction.

Other paths near this walk. Paths just N and W of Llyn Morynion seem to have gone, and the path NW from the road at 743 419 is reedy and hard to follow.

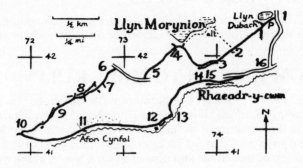

Note that walks 34 and 35 can be joined using a scenic streamside path. At stage 10 of walk 34, cross bridge and turn L along by stream. Turn L along lane, L over bridge, R along lane. Fork R to pass church. At farm fork R along lane and follow stage 11.

A FEW MORE WALKS

These have been adapted from the lower sections of some of the walks in my earlier book 'Walks in the Snowdonia Mountains'.

FROM GERLAN TO MOEL FABAN

(6 km, 3¾ mi, 1000 ft) is a pleasant walk, but stage 7 is rather featureless. Parking: if on the A5 going N, take first R turn (627 660) at the outskirts of Bethesda. Sharp R at crossroads. Stop in second road on L, 'Stryd Morgan Street' (632 664) or nearby. **1** Go to top of this street and turn L. Soon keep on along track. **2** Turn R up lane. **3** At iron gate by house go L 30 m and bear L down to stream. Cross to iron gate. Go on along path. **4** At wall on your R turn half R to slab bridge and field corner. Then half L past house and R along lane which turns L. **5** Turn R up track. Follow wall on your L. **6** On up open hill, on over stream and crossing track. Either go up over Moel Faban to rejoin route at 7, or: find path passing L of it; after slight descent fork half R along clear crossing path gently up. When it fades join parallel small path a little R. **7** Follow path to col, where you take main path gently up, but soon fork R along level path. Cross moor roughly heading for spoil heaps on ridge. May be wet patches. Path slowly bears R. **8** After stony area, path bears R to climb ridge diagonally. **9** Turn R over stile and down ridge to next stile. Here down path gently descending side of ridge. **10** At wall go parallel

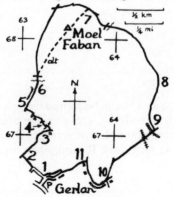

96

to it and over stile. Follow wall on your L, keeping about 10 m from it. Soon join track. **11** Turn L through iron gate soon after 2nd house. Over field to wall gap. Go on until wall forces you to the R down track between walls.

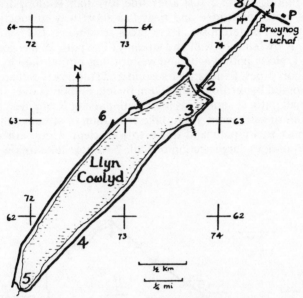

A CIRCUIT OF LLYN COWLYD

(9.5 km, 6 mi, 500 ft) may be of interest to experienced walkers. Park at Brwynog-uchaf (746 641) near the end of the narrow mountain road from above Trefriw to Llyn Cowlyd. **1** Go on along road, over bridge and soon turn L along track to centre of dam. **2** Turn L along dam and R along stony edge of lake (or over marshy ground if water level is high). **3** Join path up to gate in fence. Here cross wettish ground to join clear path seen 100 m ahead in bracken. **4** When the path fades, keep on and down rough ground to cross stream just beyond end of lake. **5** Here go up to return R along clear track. **6** At fork stay on lower path. (May need wide detour L to dodge wet area before stile.) **7** At dam follow track L up. **8** Turn R after passing under pipeline.

LLYN DULYN AND MELYNLLYN

(**9.5 km, 6 mi, 900 ft**) are remote lakes for tough walkers who like to get away from the crowd. Park at road end 732 663. **1** Turn R (NW) along track. **2** Just after stile fork half R along track. **3** Cross large footbridge and bear L a short way to junction of stream and watercourse. Here cross stream, go L 15 m, then sharp R by fence or wall and stream. (The path W has gone.) **4** Turn L along path, vague and wet at times but marked by stiles and short pipes. **5** Just after a second iron stile a very wet area can be avoided by turning L for 100 m by fence, then R over stream on small path. It soon joins main path passing R of pines. (Note remains of settlement.) **6** At lake cross dam or stream and go R up short rocky path and down to join clear wide path which climbs under a large section of wall. **7** At next lake follow track back.

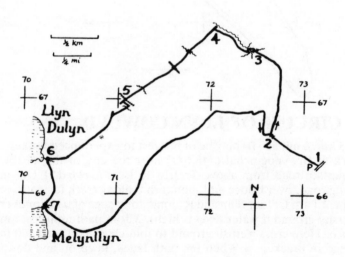

BELOW MOEL SIABOD

(8 km, 5 mi, 1400 ft) lies the attractive Llyn y Foel reached after a rocky scramble by a stream. Park just up minor road (734 571) leaving A5 just over 1.5 km (1 mi) from Capel Curig road junction, or in layby on A5. **1** Go on along minor road 400 m, then half R up stony track between house and fence. **2** Into wood, soon ignoring a sharp R turn off. Take R turn soon after this. **3** Turn R at junction. **4** When track ends go L across stream and up path in trees, with stream not far R. (Waterfall soon.) **5** Over stile out of wood along path 50 m to stream. Cross stream and follow path on R of stream. Leave stream as it bears L to a gorge. On up path. **6** Stream gets back to path, which becomes bouldery and has an easy scramble. (Avoid final wettish patch by detour R.) **7** Go on past lake to turn R along path. Soon down with heather just to your L. **8** Bear R down drive.

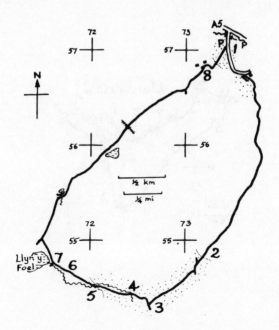

ABOVE LLANBERIS

(6 km, 3¾ mi, 800 ft) a network of paths bring you to mountain streams and fine waterfalls. If coming from top of Llanberis Pass, park by stile and footpath sign on L just before Royal Victoria Hotel on R (584 595). **1** Go along the stony track which winds and narrows. **2** Turn L up road. At road bend, turn R along path with wall on your L. Later cross railway. (Falls on R.) **3** 100 m before ruin bear R along path to cross bridge and keep on (NW). **4** Turn R along track. Ignore turnings on the R. **5** Turn L at T-junction. After bends R and then L turn very sharp R down path. **6** Bear slightly R as you pass L of small girder framework. Soon leave path and make for gate. Cross road and go along track passing just L of buildings. **7** Bear R along road 150 m then keep on along path by wall on your L. Soon turn L along path through gate and R beside wall (on your R). **8** Bear R between buildings and along track. (Falls near railway.) **9** At road turn R under railway, then L, then R.

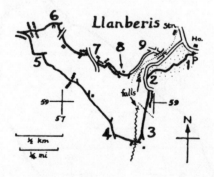

A WATKIN WALK

(6.5 km, 4 mi, 900 ft) below Snowdon is simple and rewarding. Park at Bethania car park (628 507) on the A498 5 km (3 mi) NE of Beddgelert. **1** Cross bridge and turn sharp R along drive. **2** Fork half L up track. **3** At top of rise (after passing waterfalls) turn L up path and soon R along embankment top. **4** Bear R to pass mine ruins (kept on your L). Soon join track back. **5** When back at 'top of rise' try crossing stream to vary descent, but get back to the other side using slate bridge.

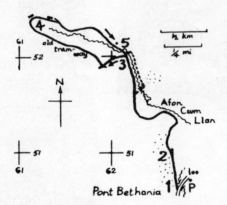

More walking books from Gwasg Carreg Gwalch

Walks on the Llŷn Peninsula

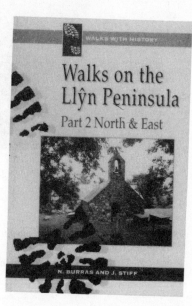

Walks in Pembrokeshire

Send for our full colour catalogue:
GWASG CARREG GWALCH
12 Iard yr Orsaf, Llanrwst, Dyffryn Conwy LL26 0EH.